# NOT FOR SALE AT ANY PRICE

## HOW WE CAN SAVE AMERICA FOR OUR CHILDREN

# ROSS PEROT

HYPERION

**NEW YORK**

ISBN 1-56282-723-5

First Edition
10  9  8  7  6  5  4  3  2  1

# United We Stand America Mission Statement

*"We the people of
United We Stand America,
recognizing that our republic
was founded as a government
of the people, by the people
and for the people, unite to
restore the integrity of our
economic and political systems.
We commit ourselves to organize,
to educate, to participate in
the political process, and to hold
our public servants accountable.
We shall rebuild our country,
renew its economic, moral and
social strength, and return the
sovereignty of America
to her people."*

We, The People, have
something more important
than
the lobbyists' money.

## WE HAVE THE VOTE!

**Working together as a team,
in United We Stand America
we can take back our country.**

*— Ross Perot*

# Contents

# Acknowledgments

This book is dedicated to millions of great Americans who organized themselves and created a new organization to rebuild our country and pass the American Dream on to our children.

◆　◆　◆　◆　◆

I would like to single out Mike Poss for special recognition for his outstanding creative work.

I would also like to thank Robert Pierce for the many hours spent producing the graphics for this book.

Bobbie Van Pelt did a brilliant job of typing and proofreading the many versions of the manuscript.

Chris Hansen worked diligently to locate and verify the data.

# Foreword

The purpose of *Not for Sale at Any Price* is to examine in detail the causes and solutions to the problems that face our country. Specifically, it deals with the economic and political situations that we find ourselves in today.

If we are going to solve our economic problems, we must first reform our political system.

I would like to express my appreciation to all of you who voted — no matter how you voted — in the 1992 election. Your participation sent a message that the American people are tired of business as usual in their government. It is now time to make that message more specific. We must tell Washington exactly what the people expect from our government.

United We Stand America belongs to the people of this country. Together, our voices can be heard. You may be interested in America's reaction to United We Stand America:

- 20% of the people who responded to a recent poll say they intend to join United We Stand America;

- Twenty million people watched or heard our recent TV-Radio program on government reform;

- 89% liked the message;

- 86% want more programs of this type;

- 79% want United We Stand America to continue as a nationwide organization.

## NOT FOR SALE AT ANY PRICE

This level of support from the people is precious —
United We Stand America must re-earn it every day. It
has nothing to do with me.

All proceeds from the sale of this book go directly to
United We Stand America to be used in the effort to
return this country to its rightful owners — the citizens of
the United States.

It's time to pick up a shovel and clean out the barn!
Let's get to work.

— Ross Perot

# Chapter One

## We Own This Country

We are the luckiest people in the world.

We live in the greatest country in the history of man.

Hundreds of millions of people around the world would change places with us in a second.

History teaches us that adversity builds strength, but success breeds arrogance and complacency.

We have been so rich for so long that we now take these fragile strengths for granted.

Today, our great country is at a critical turning point. We face serious economic problems. Our elected servants have mismanaged our money. Simply put, our government no longer works the way our Founding Fathers intended.

The President, Democrats and Republicans blame one another, and nobody accepts responsibility for anything — especially the $4 trillion national debt that <u>you and I</u> now owe.

Our elected officials seldom talk about the fact that we are the most violent, crime-ridden society in the industrialized world. Neither do they talk about the fact that we have the least effective school systems in the industrialized world. They certainly don't talk about the fact that we are shipping entire industries overseas and destroying millions of jobs. We will discuss all that and more in this book.

Nobody in Washington accepts responsibility for the problems our country faces. People in government never just look you in the eye and say, "I made a mistake." They look for fall guys and create massive cover-ups. Then they spend millions of our dollars on special prosecutors, who are accountable to no one, trying to determine whose fault it was.

Placing the blame on Washington, however, is too easy. If we really want to know who is responsible for the mess we're in, all we have to do is look in the mirror. You and I own this country, and we are responsible for what happens to it.

As owners of this country, we have made a critical mistake. We have taken our eye off the cash register, and an owner simply can't afford to do that. In the system we have today, the citizen — an owner of this country — can't even get his hands on the federal cash register. The average citizen  has no voice because of the way our government is structured. The government cash register that holds our tax money is controlled by political action committees and individuals who contribute thousands, or even millions of dollars to political campaigns.

Unfortunately, the strongest hands on the cash register are those of the foreign lobbyists and the special interests who spend millions of dollars each year to influence politics. This is the primary reason we are losing our industrial base.

# WE OWN THIS COUNTRY

The average hardworking taxpayer has no way to make his voice heard. He just doesn't have the money to get the attention of the people he elects.

To correct the situation, we must all join together as owners of this great country to

- Reform our government
- Rebuild our country
- Stop spending our children's money
- Pay off our debts
- Make certain that the next century will be the greatest in our country's history

By achieving the first goal — reforming government — the remaining goals will fall into place. The biggest obstacle to government reform is the money that is spread around by the foreign and domestic lobbyists, the political action committees, and others with special access to key officials. The American people must demand an end to the influence-peddling of these special interests.

We need a fundamental change in our government. We, the owners, must erect large signs in front of Congress, the White House, and every government office that read **NOT FOR SALE AT ANY PRICE**.

# Chapter Two

## Under the Hood

After going $4 trillion in debt, it would be reasonable to expect that we had solved all of our problems — other than paying off the huge debt we had accumulated while buying Utopia. You would think we had just bought the best schools, best health care system, and best infrastructure that money could buy. But we didn't. Instead, we have high dropout rates that lead to high crime rates. We have homeless people. We have an expensive health care system that cannot deliver the services demanded of it, and we have deteriorating bridges, highways, and tunnels.

We — the people — have to fix the problems and pay off the debt, and that's a double burden. But there's no other recourse; we have to do it. Let's not waste time complaining and witch-hunting. Let's get to work.

As tough as this job may appear, it is nothing when compared to the struggle that faced our ancestors during the American Revolution. I would much rather have this task than the challenge the pioneers faced going West. There is just one question — are we as strong and tough as they were? Of course we are. Let's show the world that the American spirit is still alive and well. If millions of us will work together, we can solve these problems.

At a time when our government has an adversarial relationship with American business, our international competitors have governments that have an intelligent, supportive relationship with business. We need long-term thinking. We need to target growth industries of the future, and make certain the words "Made in the USA" are proudly displayed on the products of the future. We need to have the most rapidly growing small business sector in the world, because more jobs can be created more quickly in this arena than any other. All of this is possible, but if you examine the laws and regulations handcuffing American businesses, I think you'll conclude that we're going at it the wrong way.

In addition, our government is still organized to focus on and fight the Cold War, even though it's over. We must commit our government to rebuild America and to rebuild our job base. A growing, expanding job base gives us a growing, expanding tax base. That is the only way we can pay off the debt and fix the problems that demand attention.

We must realize that the twenty-first century will be driven by capitalism around the world. Unfortunately, most people in Washington do not understand capitalism, business, or creating jobs. Over the years, they've become experts at passing laws, collecting taxes, raising taxes, creating bureaucracy, raising huge amounts of money for campaigns, and cashing in with a high-paying job at the end of their service. Or, in the worst case, they benefit from a very high-priced retirement plan that is several multiples of what an average worker receives. It is a strange phenomenon that our servants in Washington have much better retirement plans than we do.

Capitalism is not static; it's dynamic. It changes over time. The people in Washington believe that capitalism is fixed like a block of granite. They believe it cannot be changed. Capitalism is not like a piece of granite; it is like clay to be molded to meet the current needs of a country and its people. Germany and Japan learned capitalism after World War II. Their capitalism is focused on creating high-paying jobs for the future, and they have done it superbly. In the 1950s, the wages of our factory workers were several times greater than those of Japan and Germany. We now trail Germany, and Japan is only slightly behind. Who's winning and who's losing?

Believe it or not, Washington is still worried about our companies becoming too large, even though some of our largest corporations are shrinking in size and laying off tens of thousands of people each month. We must rethink the relationship between business and government in this country to be assured that the needs of the people of the United States are met in the twenty-first century. Clinging to our old policies is a losing proposition.

We all want a country that is a model for the rest of the world. In order to have such a country, we must be an economic superpower. If we are broke, we cannot be a superpower and we cannot be a force for good throughout the world. If you question this statement, just look at the former Soviet Union. Unless the United States is the world's leading manufacturer, we cannot be a superpower. We are losing manufacturing jobs to the rest of the world in large numbers. We must make products here. They must be the finest products in the world. If they are not, other people from other countries will not buy them, and our own people won't buy them. If you question that, look at the cars on any parking lot. But we can fix that. Here's what we have to do — we are going to have to outthink, outcreate, and outwork everybody else in the world.

Now, that can be fun if we will just do it. We won't have any time for hate or divisiveness. We must all stick together in a united team. We are a melting pot. We come from many places. That's a strength, but we've turned it into a weakness. We must turn it back into a strength. Our diversity is a great strength. United teams win; divided teams lose. That's why we call our organization United We Stand America. Our organization is made up of millions of people who are willing to make the sacrifices necessary to pass on the American Dream to our children. Our goal is to see that the United States remains the finest, strongest, and kindest country in the world.

We once had the world's greatest economic engine. We let it slip away, and with it went millions of jobs and taxpayers. Let's get under the hood and figure out what happened to the engine. We'll diagnose the problem, but I can tell you before we start that an engine tune-up won't fix it. We're going to have to do a major overhaul.

## Soaring Federal Debt

The graph on page 17 indicates that at the end of fiscal year 1992 our total federal debt was over $4 trillion. Look at its growth since 1975. We must stop spending more than we take in, or it will destroy our country. To give you a sense of how rapidly our debt has grown, look

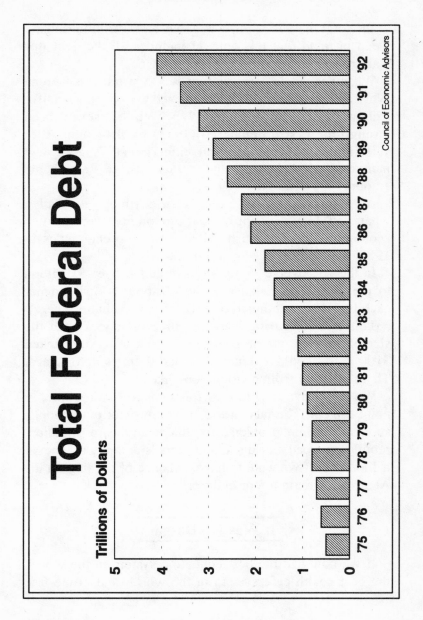

at the total in 1975 — it was about half a trillion dollars. Keep in mind that this amount includes all the debt this country has incurred from 1776 to 1976.

We managed to pay for two world wars, the Korean War, and the Vietnam War and yet we only had half a trillion dollars of debt in 1975. We had even been through the first oil embargo (1973) by that time. After suffering through another oil embargo (1979), we had increased our debt to — what was then an unthinkable amount — $1 trillion by 1981.

As it turned out, we hadn't seen anything yet. Call it what you like — supply-side economics, trickle-down economics, George Bush called it voodoo economics in 1980 — whatever it was, it didn't work.

In the last twelve years we have added over $3 trillion to the debt. This is an average of about $1 trillion per each four-year administration. Do you see a pattern here?

This is a staggering load for our economy. To put the size of the debt into perspective, a stack of tightly packed $100 bills would extend over 3,200 miles into space. That's what $4 trillion would look like.

We don't have time to look for scapegoats, or whine, or point fingers. The facts are that we must fix our schools, solve the crime problem, fix the health care situation, rebuild our roads, bridges, and tunnels and pay off the $4 trillion debt if we want to have a chance of passing on the American Dream to our children.

## It Was No Bargain

If we now had the best education system in the world, the best health care system in the world, and crime-free cities, then a $4 trillion debt might be tolerable. We wouldn't be in need of much else, so we could work on paying the interest and paying down the principal.

Instead, we have the debt with very little to show for it. What would $4 trillion have bought us?

Take a look at the map on page 20 and notice the states that appear darker. Four trillion dollars will buy —

- A $100,000 home for every family in those states, and
- A $10,000 car for every family in those states, and
- One thousand hospitals at $10 million each, and
- Two thousand schools at $10 million each.

Then we could take the money that's leftover, and just the interest on that amount would be enough to —

- Pay 40,000 nurses a salary of $32,760 per year, and
- Pay 40,000 teachers a salary of $32,760 per year, and
- Give every family a $5,000 annual bonus.

## President Clinton's Plan

If you think $4 trillion would have bought a lot, just think what $5 trillion would buy. That's where the debt will be in 1996 under President Clinton's proposed financial plan according to the Congressional Budget Office. Even after the proposed tax increases and spending cuts, President Clinton's plan will add another $1 trillion to the debt during the next four years. This assumes, among other things, that no emergencies arise, that interest rates remain relatively low, and that health care reform can be implemented at no cost to the taxpayer.

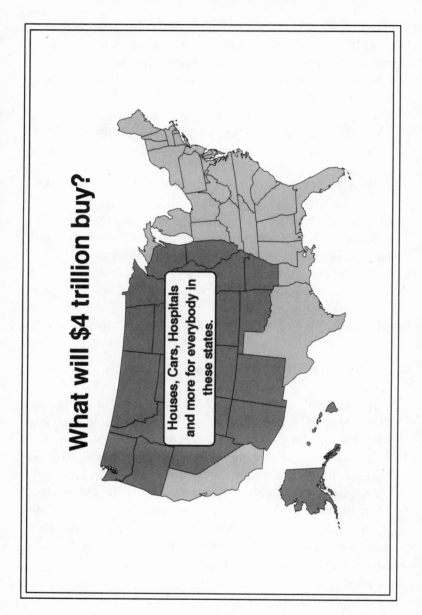

# UNDER THE HOOD

Both the House of Representatives and the Senate have approved President Clinton's fiscal 1994 budget blueprint containing about $1.5 trillion in spending and about $1.24 trillion in revenue. This places the estimated deficit at $253.5 billion for the fiscal year ending on September 30, 1994. This vote was only a resolution. The more difficult votes will come later in 1993 when Congress must decide upon specific proposals for tax increases and spending cuts that are assumed in President Clinton's proposal.

The House resolution calling for $1.24 trillion in revenue assumes that President Clinton's proposed tax increases will be enacted. Those proposals call for an energy tax, raising the top income tax bracket to 36% for corporations and on individuals with taxable incomes above $115,000, and increasing to 85% from 50% the amount of Social Security benefits that are subject to taxation for recipients with outside income of more than $25,000 for individuals and $32,000 for married couples.

The one item that was not contained in the resolution was a health care reform package. The administration is still formulating the plan at this time. It is certain to contain changes in the way health care services are delivered and additional tax increases to cover those Americans who currently have no health care coverage. Health care reform is shaping up to be one of the most important tests for the Clinton administration. We'll take a more detailed look at health care costs later in this chapter.

Immediately after passing the budget resolution, the House also passed President Clinton's short-term economic stimulus plan that provides $16.3 billion in new appropriations. This bill is defined as an emergency spending measure, and the outlays will be added to the fiscal 1993 budget deficit. The plan is designed to create up to one million jobs in the next two years. Whether these one-time, one-project jobs can revitalize the economy remains to be seen. The bill also contains $4 billion in extended unemployment benefits for the long-term jobless.

Now, in fairness to the President, no one is seriously suggesting that a financial plan could be introduced that would stop deficit spending immediately and not add any additional debt to the $4 trillion pile that we already have. The problem is that the proposed financial plan doesn't adequately address the issues of the debt and the deficit in the long-term. Even with the large tax increases that are being proposed, we will still have large deficits on the scale of the previous twelve years. This has to tell you that we're in for some major spending increases. Any serious attempt at controlling the deficit must include some major spending cuts along with tax increases.

## Stop the Bleeding

The official figure has us $4 trillion in debt, but let's take a look at page 23. The total obligations of the United States government are actually around $15 trillion. This is why we can't keep running these annual budget deficits. This is not like the depression in the 1930s when we didn't have government guarantees. We have a total of $15 trillion guaranteed by the United States taxpayers. These guarantees cover banks, savings and loans, pension funds, home mortgages, and more. If our economy ever comes off the track and these guarantees kick in, our

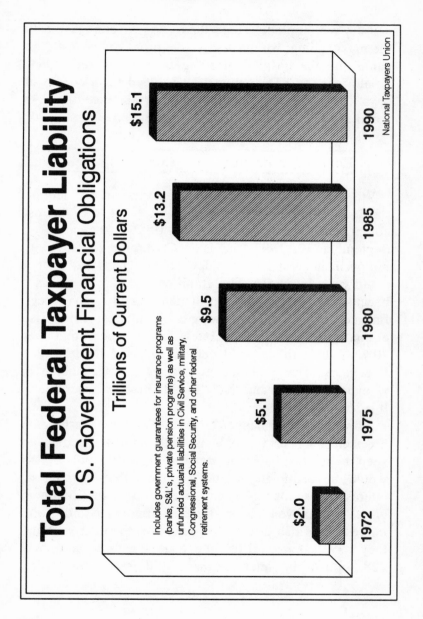

# Total Federal Taxpayer Liability
## U. S. Government Financial Obligations

Trillions of Current Dollars

Includes government guarantees for insurance programs (banks, S&L's, private pension programs) as well as unfunded actuarial liabilities in Civil Service, military, Congressional, Social Security, and other federal retirement systems.

$2.0 — 1972
$5.1 — 1975
$9.5 — 1980
$13.2 — 1985
$15.1 — 1990

National Taxpayers Union

country will implode. That's the reason we can't just keep the music going; we must solve the problems now. If you came into the hospital bleeding from a severed artery, would you say, "Doctor, just let it bleed for a couple of days?" No. You would say, "Let's stop the bleeding." As a nation, that's what we must do right now.

## Long-term Problems — Short-term Debt

We've talked about the principal portion of our debt — the $4 trillion — so now let's look at the interest component. During fiscal year 1992 that ended on September 30, 1992, the U.S. Government paid $199 billion in interest on the federal debt. That's bad, but it could get a lot worse. The graph on page 25 shows that, because of the manner in which our debt has been financed, we are at great risk if interest rates rise dramatically, or even moderately. The reason is that over 70% of the publicly held debt is financed for less than five years. That's suicide in business, that's suicide in your personal life, and that's suicide in your government. It is irresponsible.

How did this happen? The folks in Washington financed long-term problems with short-term debt to keep the interest payments down so that the annual deficit would be artificially reduced. That's fine as long as interest rates don't rise. But if rates rise, the debt will grow larger even faster. Let's assume that short-term interest rates rise just one percent over the next year and they stay at that level for five years. That's an additional $28 billion in interest that we'll owe each year.

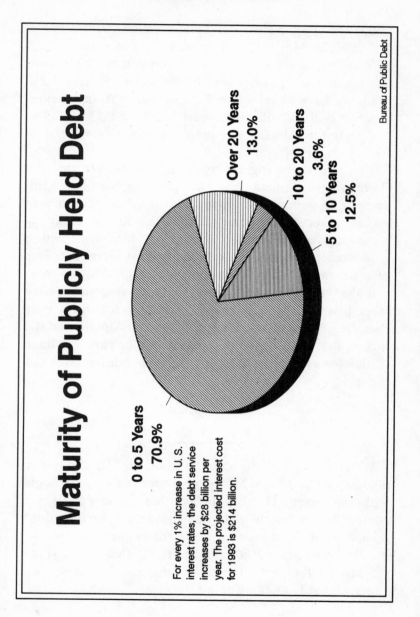

## Maturity of Publicly Held Debt

**0 to 5 Years
70.9%**

For every 1% increase in U. S.
interest rates, the debt service
increases by $28 billion per
year. The projected interest cost
for 1993 is $214 billion.

**Over 20 Years
13.0%**

**10 to 20 Years
3.6%**

**5 to 10 Years
12.5%**

Bureau of Public Debt

# NOT FOR SALE AT ANY PRICE

In April 1993, a five-year Treasury note yields a return of 5.2%. In May 1982, five-year Treasury notes paid 13.7%. During the next five years, do you think it's more likely that interest rates will be between 0% and 5.2% when we have to refinance 70% of the debt, or whether they more likely will be between 5.2% and 13.7%? The prospects for reducing the interest payments on our debt are not promising.

It's particularly frightening when you realize that the German government has to pay almost four full percentage points more than the United States does to borrow short-term money. The reason Germany is borrowing heavily right now is to pay for infrastructure improvements to what was formerly East Germany. This need for capital by the Germans will not go away soon.

If the Japanese, the Germans, the Arabs, and all the other investors who buy U.S. Treasury securities ever lose confidence in the United States of America or the U.S. dollar, we will be in serious trouble. This is a huge burden for us to bear. We can't pass this burden on to our children.

## Deficit ≠ Debt

We've discussed the debt in some detail, and we've mentioned the deficit. Maybe it's because they both begin with the letter "D," but I find that some people get confused between the debt and the deficit, or they don't realize what the deficit is. It's actually pretty simple — it's disappointing, but it's simple. The deficit is one year's increase in the debt. The chart on page 27 shows you exactly what I'm talking about.

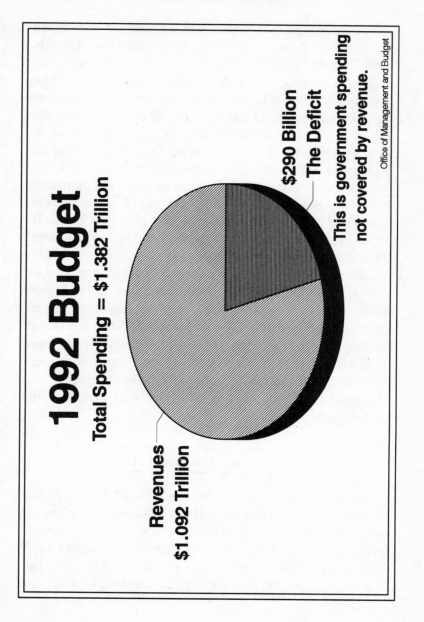

# NOT FOR SALE AT ANY PRICE

The entire pie represents the amount of money our government spent during 1992. It was about $1.4 trillion. The lighter portion indicates that the government collected revenue (taxes, fees, etc.) of about $1.1 trillion. The darker portion represents the difference between the amount we spent and the amount we collected, which is the budget deficit for 1992. The excess spending — the deficit — is paid for by borrowing from investors in this country and overseas. The national debt of $4 trillion is simply the accumulation of all the annual deficits that we have incurred over the years, less any debt repayments from budget surpluses. The deficit of $290 billion in 1992 increased the debt from $3.8 trillion to a total of $4.1 trillion.

During the years when we take in more money than we spend, a budget surplus occurs and the debt is paid down. Unfortunately, we have only had a budget surplus in one of the last thirty-three years — 1969. No one in Washington tells you that we can't keep running up these deficits, and that the debt is destroying our country and our children's future. That's proof that we need an electronic town hall meeting. We must keep an eye on the cash register.

## Where Does It Come From?

We just mentioned that we took in $1.1 trillion last year from taxes, fees, and other sources. The chart on page 29 shows that $476 billion came from personal income taxes, $414 billion came from FICA taxes, $100 billion came from income taxes on corporations, $46 billion came from excise taxes (tires, cigarettes, etc.), and

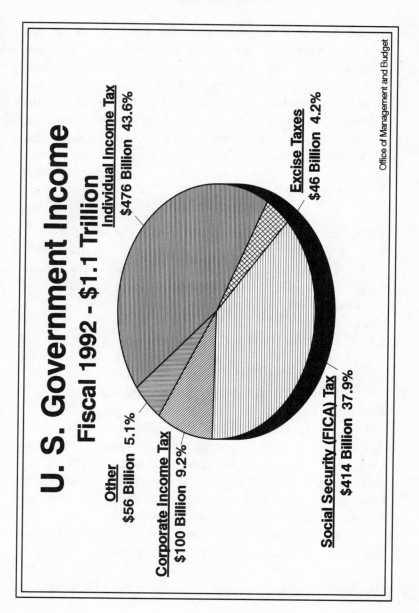

U. S. Government Income

Fiscal 1992 - $1.1 Trillion

Individual Income Tax
$476 Billion   43.6%

Other
$56 Billion   5.1%

Corporate Income Tax
$100 Billion   9.2%

Excise Taxes
$46 Billion   4.2%

Social Security (FICA) Tax
$414 Billion   37.9%

Office of Management and Budget

$56 billion came from fees and other taxes. I thought this was an interesting graph because I found one day while visiting with some senior officials in Washington that they didn't have a clear picture of where the money to run the government was coming from. I wanted to know, and I thought you should know, too. Keep in mind that the top sources of revenue, by far, are the income taxes and social insurance taxes (FICA) paid by individuals.

## Where Does It Go?

The graph on page 31 shows us that the single biggest government expenditure is $728 billion for "entitlements" — Social Security, Medicare, Medicaid, and other social programs. It is more than one-half the entire budget of our government. It dwarfs everything else. Even a quick glance at this graph and the graph on page 29 will tell you that we're paying out a lot more for entitlement programs than we're getting from the collection of Social Security taxes. The simple fact is that it will be difficult to ever balance the budget until we deal with the dilemmas imposed by entitlement programs. We'll be talking more about these problems later in the book.

The second largest expenditure is for national defense. Last year we spent $298 billion, or almost 22% of our total outlays, for defense. We'll discuss an idea later in this book for reducing defense spending without damaging the effectiveness of the military.

The next largest expenditure is for — this might make you sick — interest expense on the debt. This huge expense would have been even higher had it not been for the questionable practice of short-term financing at

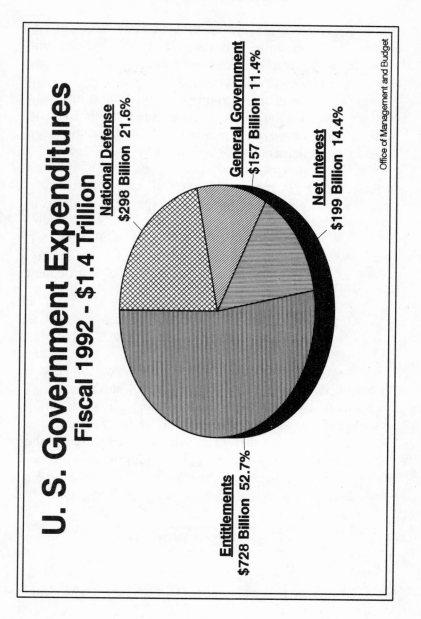

# U. S. Government Expenditures
## Fiscal 1992 - $1.4 Trillion

**National Defense**
$298 Billion 21.6%

**General Government**
$157 Billion 11.4%

**Net Interest**
$199 Billion 14.4%

**Entitlements**
$728 Billion 52.7%

Office of Management and Budget

relatively low interest rates. We spent $199 billion of our money for something that didn't buy us anything this year. Interest payments alone were equal to 14.4% of our total expenditures for the year.

Here's an interesting phenomenon. We hear a lot about the amount of waste in our government agencies, and correctly so. However, when we look at the amount we spend on entitlements, defense, and interest, it looks like general government operations are a bargain at $157 billion. Don't get me wrong, we still need to eliminate fraud, waste, abuse, and pork-barrel spending in all areas of government. I'm just pointing out that we couldn't solve the deficit problem even if we eliminated all functions of the government other than entitlements, defense, and interest. Let's look at the entitlement programs.

## How Entitlements Grow

Do we really have to worry about the projected growth in our obligations for entitlements? The graph on page 33 suggests that we had better do something. If we don't, by the year 2020 the cost of Social Security, Medicare, Medicaid, and the other entitlements is projected to be $1.8 trillion a year. Now, keep in mind, our total income today from all sources is only $1.1 trillion a year. We must develop a plan to deal with our future obligations.

## How the Deficit Will Grow

If entitlements cost us $1.8 trillion in the year 2020, how large will that make the deficit in the same year?

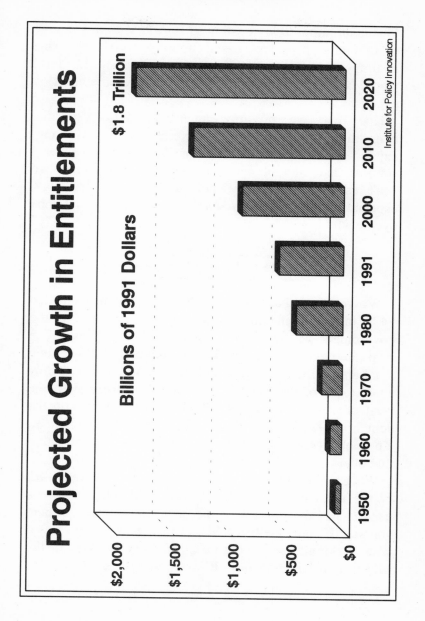

Projected Growth in Entitlements

Billions of 1991 Dollars

$1.8 Trillion

Institute for Policy Innovation

33

# NOT FOR SALE AT ANY PRICE

This is an impossible question to answer with any degree of certainty, however, based upon several reasonable assumptions, a guess is that the deficit (not the debt) would be $1.5 trillion in the year 2020. See the chart on page 35.

How can we possibly finance a deficit of that magnitude? One solution, of course, is to have a growing, expanding economy capable of producing the revenue to support that kind of spending and borrowing. But we can't assume that we'll have that kind of economy, especially when we keep sending our good-paying jobs overseas.

## Taxes to Pay the Interest

We've seen that in 1992 the government collected $476 billion in income taxes, and we've seen that the government paid $199 billion in interest expense. The map on page 36 will make the impact of these two numbers perfectly clear. It took an amount approximately equal to all of the income taxes collected from everyone west of the Mississippi River to pay the interest on the debt in 1992. This is totally unacceptable management. You and I would fire the management of a corporation that operated in this manner.

What is the likelihood, that after another ten years, *all* of the income taxes collected from individuals will be used to pay the interest on the debt? "That can't happen, you say. If someone had told you in 1980 that by 1992 it would take all the income taxes of everyone west of the Mississippi River to pay the interest on the debt, what

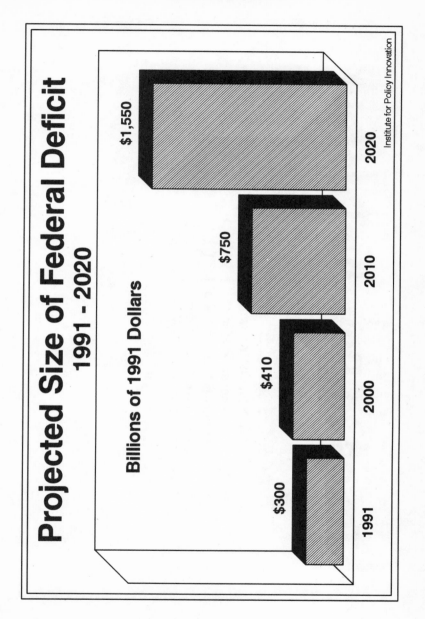

35

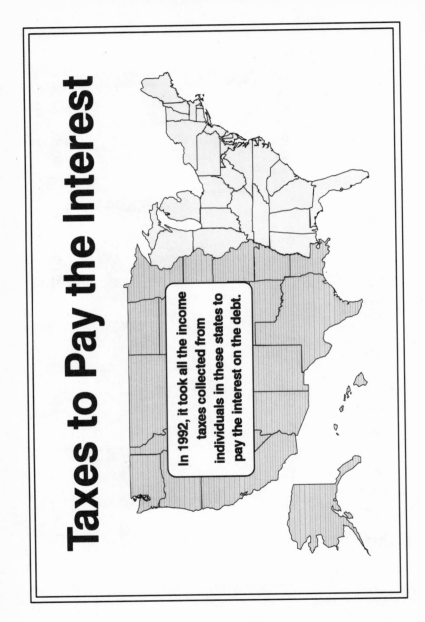

Taxes to Pay the Interest

In 1992, it took all the income taxes collected from individuals in these states to pay the interest on the debt.

would you have said? (In 1980, we collected $244 billion in taxes and we paid $53.5 billion in interest expense.)

If you're still not certain that all of our income taxes could one day be needed to pay the interest on the debt, consider this: If revenue from income taxes continues to increase at the same rate that it has increased for the last five years (3.95%), we will collect about $700 billion in 2002. If we continue to run deficits at the same pace as the last five years (11.72%), the debt will be about $12 trillion in 2002. If the average interest rate paid on the debt is 5.8% in 2002, we will pay about $700 billion in interest in 2002.

Even if you don't think it's likely to happen, you might admit it's possible. And if you're willing to admit that it's at least possible, can there be anything more important than taking the necessary and basic steps to keep it from happening?

## Percent of GNP for the Federal Government

As long as we're looking into the future, let's look at where federal spending might be in the year 2020, given a reasonable set of assumptions. The graph on page 38 indicates that twenty-seven years from now federal government spending might be about 41% of the gross national product. The government is currently spending 25% of the GNP, and in 1950 government spending only accounted for 16% of the total GNP.

I would like to think that 25% of the GNP is the highest percentage government spending would reach, and that we could begin to get the percentage back down to where it was in 1950. However, it looks like there is a

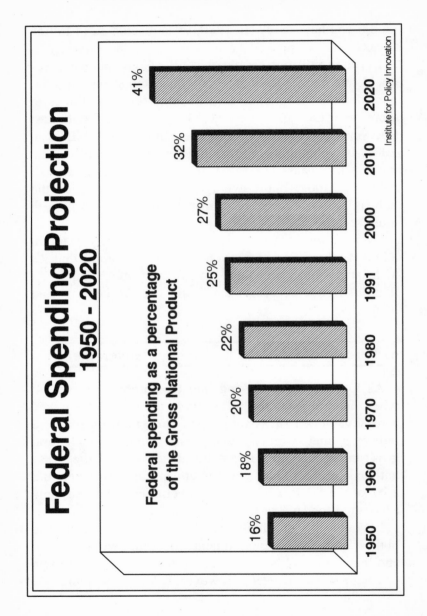

trend here, and I don't see anything being done to stop it. I mentioned earlier that we had taken our eye off the cash register. When I look at this graph, I suspect that we have put Willie Sutton in charge of the cash register. Willie Sutton was a notorious bank robber. When someone asked him why he robbed banks, he replied, "Because that's where the money is." Maybe Willie is still around, and operating inside the Washington Beltway.

## GNP Growth 1953-1992

I know that you're saying to yourself, "In a growing and expanding economy, the government can afford to spend more because there's more to go around; the pie is larger; a rising tide lifts all boats; etc., etc." In theory, I couldn't argue with you. But economists deal in theories while the rest of us have to deal with reality. If the GNP were going through the roof, maybe we could stay on the road to 41% spending by the government. However, the chart on page 40 indicates that we're not going to make it without some changes in our current economic policies.

What happened to the growth? Where did the wheels come off? I can tell you one reason for it — we got into trickle-down economics and it didn't trickle. *Trickle-down* means that the benefits of an expanding economy get down to the folks who really need the money. We'll see how far the money trickled down later in this chapter.

## Comparing Recoveries

Had President Bush seen a copy of the previous chart, maybe he would have known that we were in a recession.

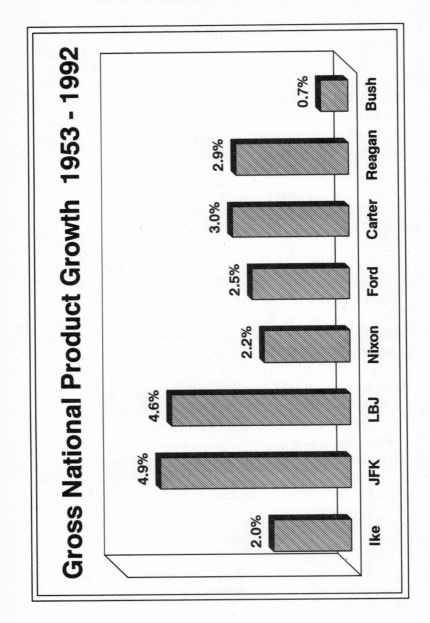

Gross National Product Growth 1953 - 1992

| President | Growth |
|-----------|--------|
| Ike | 2.0% |
| JFK | 4.9% |
| LBJ | 4.6% |
| Nixon | 2.2% |
| Ford | 2.5% |
| Carter | 3.0% |
| Reagan | 2.9% |
| Bush | 0.7% |

# UNDER THE HOOD

As it was, we kept hearing that we weren't in a recession even though the people knew we were. Later, we began to hear that we were coming out of the recession.

Let's see if we're really coming out of the recession that we were never really supposed to have been in. The chart on page 42 shows the patterns of three leading indicators during the first fifteen months after the start of a recovery. If you compare the recovery from our most recent recession with the recoveries from four previous recessions, I think you will conclude that the current recovery has left the patient anemic.

Of the three indicators — Consumer Spending, Payroll Employment, and Industrial Production — the one that really hits home is the middle bar — Payroll Employment. Notice that in previous recoveries, employment was up anywhere from just below 4% to almost 6%. In this recovery, it hasn't even hit 1%. Notice also that Industrial Production normally jumps way up compared to the other two indicators. We haven't had that sudden surge associated with previous recoveries.

I believe our government is out of touch. When I look at this chart, I think of the meat packer in Iowa I read about on the front page of the *New York Times*. He's a good man, a middle-aged man, who said, "I didn't quit my job, my job quit me." The meat packing plant closed. He was a proud man who had never taken anything from anybody. He had to go on welfare, and it hurt his pride.

One night my wonderful wife came to bed crying, and I asked, "What's the matter?" She said that she had been watching a story about a steelworker in Pittsburgh who lost his job because the steel plant had closed. He now had a minimum wage job, but he could not afford a safety inspection for his car. He needed transportation because

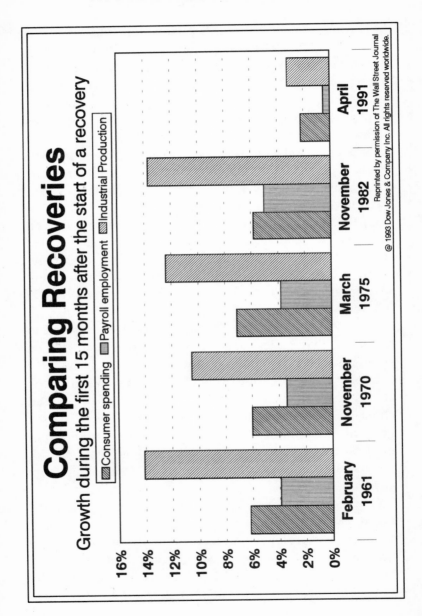

Comparing Recoveries

Growth during the first 15 months after the start of a recovery

Consumer spending  Payroll employment  Industrial Production

February
1961

November
1970

March
1975

November
1982

April
1991

Reprinted by permission of The Wall Street Journal
© 1993 Dow Jones & Company Inc. All rights reserved worldwide.

his wife was ill. It broke my wife's heart because here was a proud man who was caught up in a hurricane that he couldn't do anything about.

I mentioned earlier that we need an electronic town hall. Let me emphasize that, like the town hall meetings of the colonial days, the electronic town hall has to have two-way communications. When the people are hurting, Washington needs to know it.

## Downsizing

Does it come as any surprise, as our manufacturing plants are closed down and our workers are laid off, that our corporate profits are also down? If the corporations and businesses of a country are making money, they can spend that money on new plants, new equipment, and research. These expenditures, in turn, create new jobs that create more money to reinvest, and the cycle repeats itself. Unfortunately, today the buzzword for American business is "downsizing."

The chart on page 44 tracks U.S. corporate profits back to 1971. Notice how profits are just drifting downward from their peak in 1979. Why are profits down? Because we're getting our heads kicked in by international competitors, that's why. I had a fellow stop me one day and say, "Ross, we used to have the biggest banks in the world. How come the biggest banks in the world are now in Japan?" I said, "It's really pretty simple. The Japanese make better products than we do. We bought their products with what used to be our money. What used to be our money is now in their banks. What used to be their products are now in our homes getting

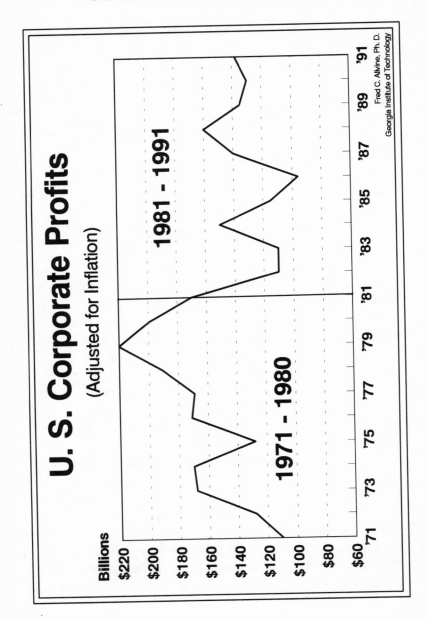

U. S. Corporate Profits

(Adjusted for Inflation)

1981 - 1991

1971 - 1980

Fred C. Allvine, Ph. D.
Georgia Institute of Technology

less valuable every day. But, what used to be our money is now in their banks getting more valuable every day."

What's wrong with shipping manufacturing jobs overseas and just becoming a service economy? Look around. We have done that for the last twelve years, and most of the jobs created here during that time were low-paying jobs. These jobs just can't support families, and they don't support our country. We've got to get back to building and making things.

In the words of a man from Japan who really sees us as a friend, "In Japan we make things; in the United States you just play with money." Think back to the late 1980s when we had the savings and loan scandals, the banking problems, and the junk bond mess. The man from Japan is right, we were just like little children playing with money. Did our government step in and stop it? No. Did anybody try to stop it? No. It was the "Bonfire of the Vanities" and "The Predators' Ball" in one lurid scene. We'll be picking up the tab for that party for a long time. Yes, it's true that some people were caught and went to prison. But, does it ever cross your mind that these guys don't mind doing two-to-five and coming out with tens of millions of dollars still in their bank accounts?

## U. S. Unemployment Rate

If we're downsizing our major industrial firms, the unemployment rate is probably rising. That conclusion is confirmed by the chart on page 46.

Once again, I'm afraid that we're looking at a disturbing trend without any clear-cut plan to reverse the direction. What happens to the aeronautical engineer

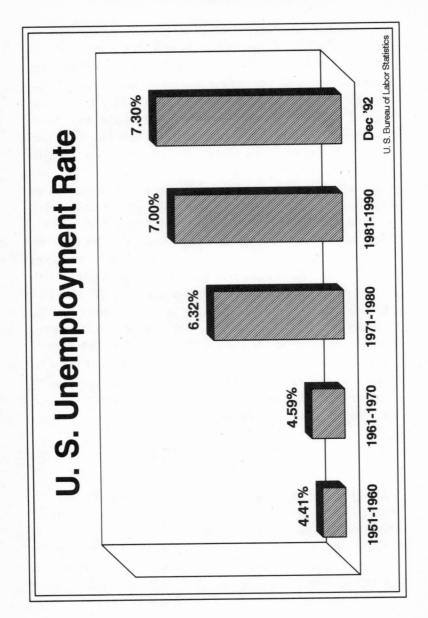

U. S. Unemployment Rate

1951-1960: 4.41%
1961-1970: 4.59%
1971-1980: 6.32%
1981-1990: 7.00%
Dec '92: 7.30%

U. S. Bureau of Labor Statistics

when a defense contract is canceled or scaled back? What happens to the banker when lending policies become so restrictive that the only people who can borrow money are the few who don't need it?

If we have experienced, hardworking people on the street, I don't have to tell you what this does for the employment chances of the recent college graduates. This year there are many wonderful young people coming out of college with good grades who can't find jobs. Even graduates from the elite business schools are having trouble finding  jobs. And God bless the kids whose parents never got a college education or maybe not even a high school education — who worked two jobs so their children could get a college degree — the American Dream may be turned into the American Disappointment for them because of unemployment.

Our friends, the Japanese, are out of workers. Wouldn't we like to have that problem. Let's go back to 1945 when they were in ashes. If I had told you that within two generations the Japanese would be out of workers, you would have laughed me out of the room.

## Jobs Lost

Because the issue of jobs is so critical to our economy, let's look at some more charts about jobs and wages to get an idea of what's happening. The chart on page 48 shows the number of corporate jobs that were lost during the four years of 1989, 1990, 1991, and 1992. We reached the high point in 1992 when we lost about 700,000 corporate jobs. We were told that things were

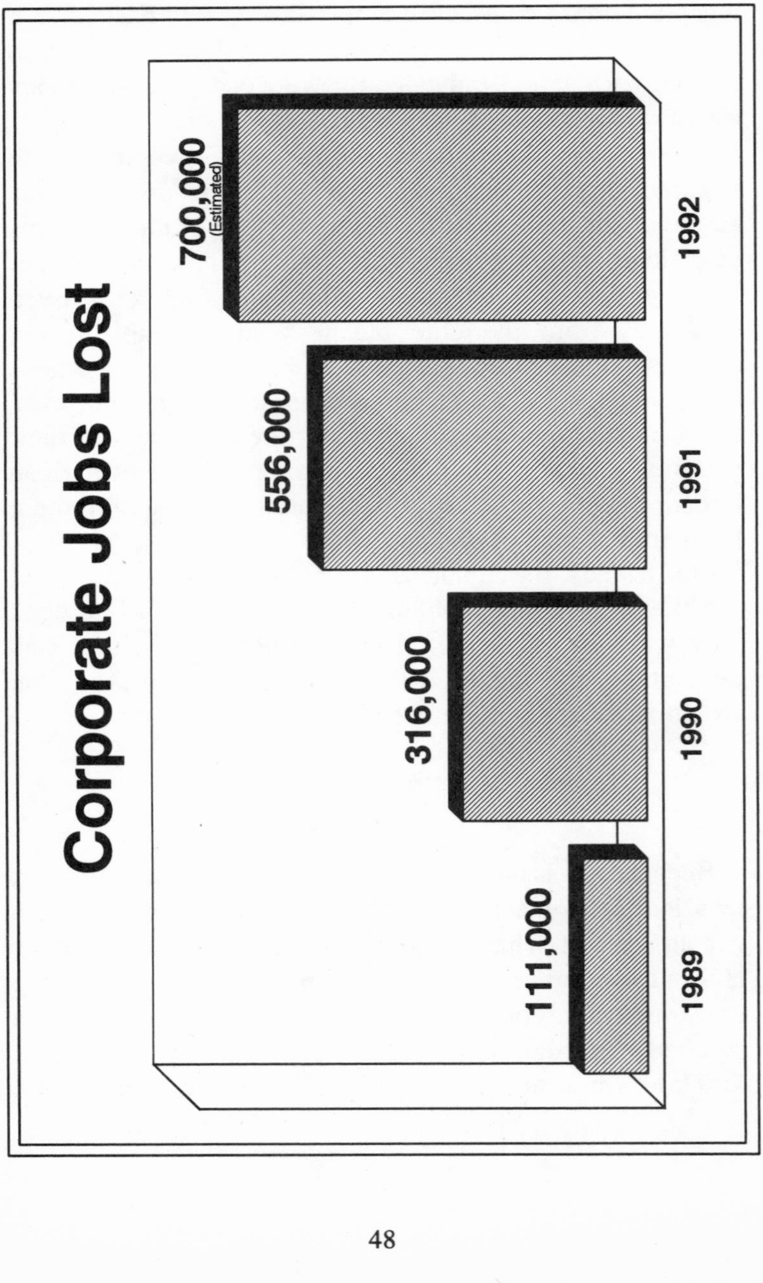

Corporate Jobs Lost

700,000 (Estimated) — 1992
556,000 — 1991
316,000 — 1990
111,000 — 1989

getting better. Do you get the idea that folks in Washington don't know what's going on? I do.

Now we might be told that these corporate jobs have been replaced with jobs in government or in the service industries, but the problem is that these new jobs don't pay as well as the corporate jobs did. The good-paying jobs got shipped overseas for reasons we'll explain later in this book.

## Wages Drop in the Eighties

Based upon what you just saw in the previous chart and upon the law of supply and demand, the information in the chart on page 50 shouldn't surprise you. The average hourly wage rate in the United States (adjusted for inflation) actually dropped during the 1980s. So not only did we have a larger percentage of people out of work, but those people who were working made less money after adjusting their income for inflation.

## Manufacturing Jobs versus Government Jobs

We have talked about the decrease in manufacturing jobs as we lose industries to our international competitors. Did you know, however, there is one sector where employment is growing fairly rapidly? It's the government sector. Before you look at the next chart, try to answer these two questions: (A) How many people in the United States work in manufacturing jobs? (B) How many people in the United States work for a branch of local, state, or federal government?

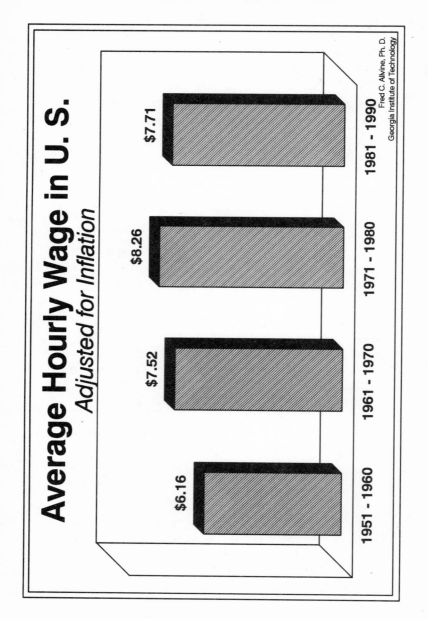

## Average Hourly Wage in U. S.
### Adjusted for Inflation

$6.16 — 1951 - 1960
$7.52 — 1961 - 1970
$8.26 — 1971 - 1980
$7.71 — 1981 - 1990

Fred C. Allvine, Ph. D.
Georgia Institute of Technology

# UNDER THE HOOD

Take a look at the chart on page 52. It shows that in 1992 we had about 19 million people working for various government entities, while at the same time we had only about 18 million people working in private sector manufacturing jobs. As the graph shows, this relationship of more government employees than private sector manufacturing employees wasn't always the case.

If we want to be a great country, we have to be a manufacturing superpower. No ifs, ands, and buts — no place to run, no place to hide. We can't be a country where the government is our primary source of new jobs, and where we're losing more manufacturing jobs than we're creating. The words "Made in the USA" can once again become the world standard for excellence, but to do it we have to reverse the trends on this chart.

Remember the chart on page 38 that showed that government spending could account for 41% of the gross national product in the year 2020? If the trend in the chart on page 52 continues, it's easy to see how we'll get to 41% — Big Government! We can't afford it.

## How Do They Do That?

If we decide to be a manufacturing superpower, we won't be able to pay our workers much money and expect to compete with the rest of the world, right? Wrong. This is Big Myth #1 coming out of Washington.

Let's look at the chart on page 53. Germany pays its workers an average of $18 an hour and has a $23 billion trade surplus. I would say that Germany is doing something right. Sweden pays its workers almost $17 an hour and has a $6 billion trade surplus. Denmark pays its

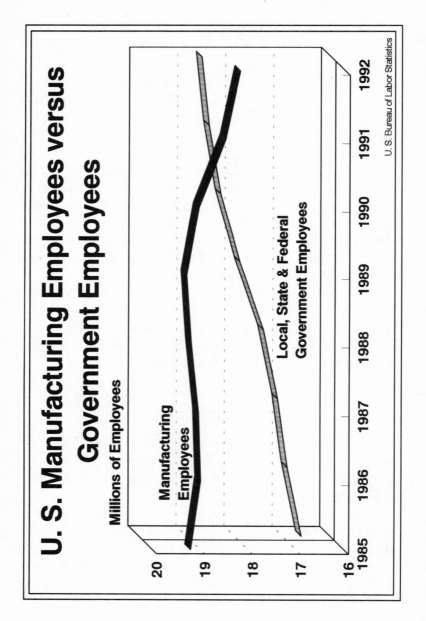

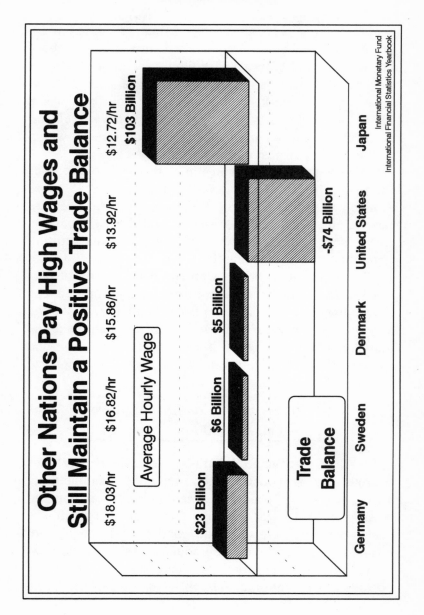

Other Nations Pay High Wages and Still Maintain a Positive Trade Balance

Average Hourly Wage

Trade Balance

| | Germany | Sweden | Denmark | United States | Japan |
|---|---------|--------|---------|---------------|-------|
| Average Hourly Wage | $18.03/hr | $16.82/hr | $15.86/hr | $13.92/hr | $12.72/hr |
| Trade Balance | $23 Billion | $6 Billion | $5 Billion | -$74 Billion | $103 Billion |

International Monetary Fund
International Financial Statistics Yearbook

workers almost $16 an hour and has $5 billion trade surplus. We pay our factory workers an average of about $14 an hour and have a $74 billion trade deficit. We are the largest debtor nation in the history of man. Finally, Japan pays its workers about $13 per hour and has a $103 billion trade surplus. We must have well-run businesses in an environment where government works with us — not against us.

If you want to know something that will break your heart — in 1950, people in our country earned 15 times as much as people in Japan. We don't anymore. They are earning almost as much as we are, and they will pass us pretty soon because they are adding manufacturing capability instead of losing it.

We can pay our workers well and have a trade surplus if we have an intelligent, supportive relationship between government and business and if our companies make the best products in the world. Our companies can make the best products in the world if we set our minds to it and we build tightly knit, united teams dedicated to winning.

## 18- to 24-Year-Olds Earning Less Than $12,000 per Year

The chart on page 55 illustrates one of the best reasons for returning our country to the status of a manufacturing superpower. The sooner we can put our experienced workers back to work at jobs that challenge them, the sooner we'll be able to create good entry-level jobs for our high school and college graduates. As it is right now, we've got older, experienced workers in jobs normally occupied by recent graduates. In 1980, 18% of the 18- to

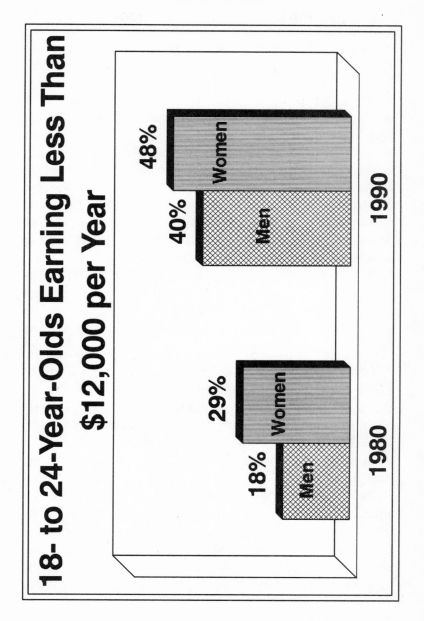

18- to 24-Year-Olds Earning Less Than $12,000 per Year

1990: Women 48%, Men 40%

1980: Women 29%, Men 18%

24 - year - old men earned less than $12,000 per year. In 1990, 40% of that same age group earned less than $12,000 per year. The situation is even worse for women. In 1980, 29% of the 18- to 24-year-old women made less than $12,000 per year. Now, that number is up to 48%. We're going backward while the rest of the world is going forward.

The 18- to 24-year-old age group actually got hammered twice. Once with the increase in the number of workers earning less than $12,000, and a second time by the drop in the purchasing power of the dollar. In a few minutes, we'll see what happened to the dollar during this period of time. Because of inflation, this group would have had to earn a lot more than $12,000 per year in 1990 just to have stayed even with the 1980 group.

## Eighteen-cent Dollar: 1950 to 1990

The chart on page 57 shows what has happened to the dollar in forty years. A dollar that used to be worth a dollar in 1950 is worth eighteen cents today. Think about the high percentage of young people who are having to begin their careers in a job paying less than $12,000 per year. No wonder both parents in many families are working — some of them at two jobs — just to make ends meet.

The value of a dollar at any point in time is based upon what it will buy. And a dollar is buying less and less and less because of the mismanagement of our country's economy. This is directly attributable to the fact that the people in Washington don't understand business. They may have understood the problems associated with the

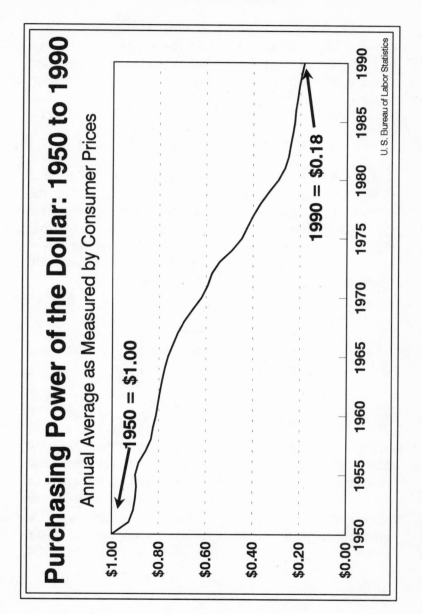

# Purchasing Power of the Dollar: 1950 to 1990

Annual Average as Measured by Consumer Prices

1950 = $1.00

1990 = $0.18

U. S. Bureau of Labor Statistics

Cold War, but our problem now is to rebuild and reindustrialize our country so we can put our people back to work. If our country is not financially strong, we are vulnerable. I believe we are vulnerable now. Do we want to leave it that way? We must not.

## Industries of the Future

If the 18- to 24-year-old group is going to have a chance at a decent living, and if we're going to stop the erosion of the value of the dollar, then we must determine the best products that we can manufacture and ship abroad. We need to identify the industries of the future and target those industries with the help (or at least with minimum interference) of our government.

The industries of the future are:

- Computer hardware
- Computer software
- Civilian aviation
- Biotechnology
- Telecommunications
- Robotics

The emerging industrial nations have already targeted these industries. The growth of their exports in recent years confirms this strategy. Take a look at the chart on page 59 to get an idea of what just a few well-chosen industries can do for the economy of a country, and what can happen to a country that lets its opportunities slip away.

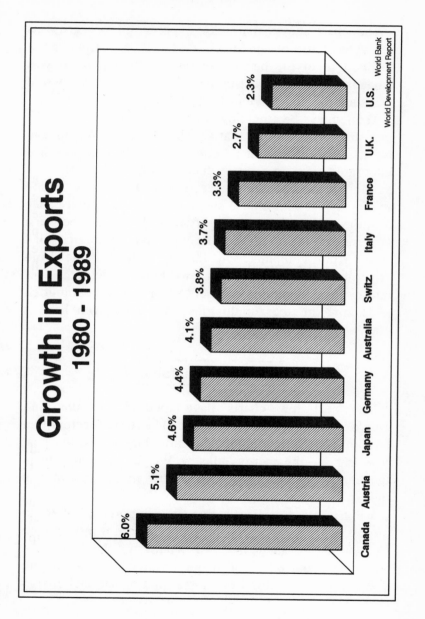

Growth in Exports
1980 - 1989

Canada 6.0%
Austria 5.1%
Japan 4.6%
Germany 4.4%
Australia 4.1%
Switz 3.8%
Italy 3.7%
France 3.3%
U.K. 2.7%
U.S. 2.3%

World Bank
World Development Report

The chart shows that U.S. exports did not grow as rapidly as those of our trading partners. In fact, we are at the bottom of the barrel. As far as exports go, it was amateur night right here in the greatest country the world has known.

You may be thinking that we already have the industries of the future that are shown above. We do, and we used to have a lot of other industries, too. We had integrated circuits, we had steel, and we had automobiles. The industries listed above are going overseas just like chips, steel, and cars did unless we develop an intelligent, supportive, relationship between government and business. These ten-year strategies don't come from companies in Japan — they come from government and business working together. Our international economic competitors are totally committed to dominating these industries. We don't even have a plan.

## We Are Vulnerable

The past few charts have focused on jobs and employment. Let's look at one of the external factors that has impacted our employment situation during the past few years — the energy industry. We've lost more jobs in the energy industry than we've lost in the automobile industry.

I don't have to tell you about the importance of oil to almost every facet of our daily lives. From transportation to clothing to medicine, we would not be the same society without oil. Even if our country had a lot of oil, you'd think we would have some kind of national energy policy. Yet, here we are twenty years after the first Arab oil embargo, and we still don't have an energy policy.

The chart on page 62 shows our dependence on foreign oil. Forty-eight percent of the oil we use is imported. We must create an energy policy. Without it, we are totally vulnerable in terms of being able to keep our factories open, keep our homes heated, keep our cars on the road, and most importantly, being able to defend ourselves. We are totally vulnerable in the event of a war. We must develop an energy policy, and we need it now.

## International Gasoline Prices and Taxes

When we talk about an energy policy — or the lack of an energy policy — one of the most important topics should be the amount of tax we pay for a gallon of gasoline. We currently pay anywhere from $92¢ to $1.20 for a gallon of regular unleaded gasoline. The price includes 35¢ per gallon for the federal government and from 7.6¢ per gallon in Georgia to 26¢ per gallon in Connecticut and Rhode Island for state government taxes.

The chart on page 63 compares these amounts with prices and taxes around the world. The Italians pay $5.10 per gallon; the French pay $4.54 per gallon; the Japanese pay $3.79 per gallon; the English pay $3.68 per gallon; and the Germans pay $3.47 per gallon. You say, "That doesn't make any sense, Ross, because the price of oil is about the same to all buyers." Yes, but look at the reason — each of those countries collects huge amounts of tax to build infrastructure and to invest in the future. In Italy the tax is $3.57 per gallon, in France it's $3.12, in Japan it's $2.25, in England it's $2.09, in Germany it's $1.99,

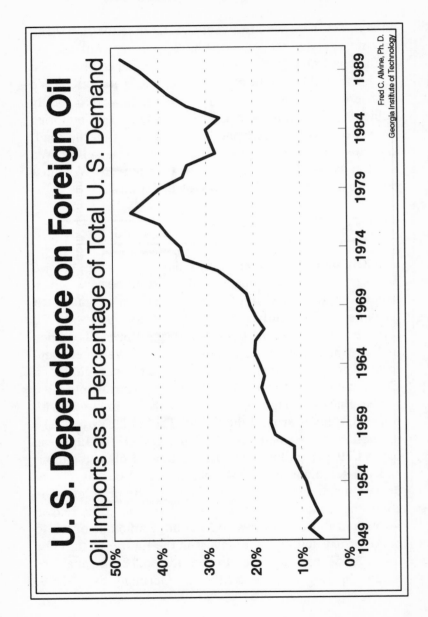

U. S. Dependence on Foreign Oil

Oil Imports as a Percentage of Total U. S. Demand

Fred C. Allvine, Ph. D.
Georgia Institute of Technology

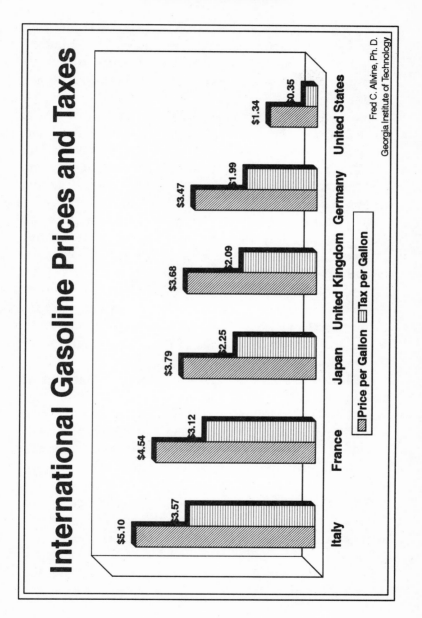

International Gasoline Prices and Taxes

| Country | Price per Gallon | Tax per Gallon |
|---|---|---|
| Italy | $5.10 | $3.57 |
| France | $4.54 | $3.12 |
| Japan | $3.79 | $2.25 |
| United Kingdom | $3.68 | $2.09 |
| Germany | $3.47 | $1.99 |
| United States | $1.34 | $0.35 |

Fred C. Allwine, Ph. D.
Georgia Institute of Technology

and in the United States it's only 35¢. Who's winning and who's losing? On the one hand you have hard-minded, committed people, and here at home we have a feel-good-now philosophy. We've got to change that if we want to win.

During the 1992 campaign, I recommended that a 50¢ per gallon tax increase be phased in over a five-year period. Conventional wisdom said that proposing an increase in the gas tax was political suicide. One element of President Clinton's economic plan is a proposed energy tax based upon the BTU content of all fuel.

After seeing the last chart, the next one on page 65 should not be a surprise. Are we investing in the future? Of course not. While we've been sitting around here in a do-nothing atmosphere, the rest of the world has been busy. Look at Japan — 16% of its gross domestic product is invested in its future. Look at Germany — 8%. Look at the United States — 4.5%. Who does tomorrow belong to? Tomorrow belongs to the people who, today, are investing in the future.

We had better get busy and start rebuilding the United States instead of just wandering around thinking that everything will just work itself out, somehow. Does that ever happen in your life — hoping that the problem will go away if you just don't confront it? If you want the problem to go away, you have to face up to it and work on it.

Why aren't we investing in the future? As one of our friends in Japan said, "In Japan we think ten years ahead, in the United States you think ten minutes ahead." He meant that in a friendly way, and I took it in a friendly way. I mention this to stir you up. We must look beyond the release of next quarter's earnings reports. We need to

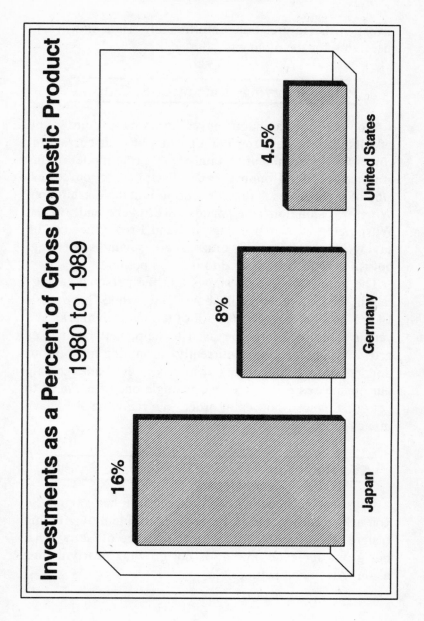

Investments as a Percent of Gross Domestic Product
1980 to 1989

16%

8%

4.5%

Japan

Germany

United States

invest in the future, but, unfortunately, right now we're just living for the moment.

## Personal Savings Rate of U. S. Citizens

"So, how does a country invest in its own future?" you ask. Its citizens have to save a portion of their current income. Our government certainly isn't a role model in this area, so we must impose some discipline on ourselves. One of my theories is that we tend to imitate Washington. When Washington overspends, we overspend. When Washington is overspending, you and I really need to be saving. Fortunately, our citizens are saving something, but it's not much compared to our competitors.

The graph on page 67 shows that the personal savings rate in the United States is about 4.1%, while Germany is 14.8% and Japan is 18.1%. All of the deutschemarks and yen in their banks can be used to help their businesses grow. Meanwhile, we're currently consuming most of our dollars, and we don't have our money in our banks to help our businesses grow. We, every single one of us, need to get our financial houses in order. We really need to have money in the bank.

## Average Annual Growth in Domestic Product

Let's face it, spending is a lot more fun than saving. So you ask, "Can we finesse the savings problem by growing faster?" I'm afraid not. The chart on page 68 shows that our gross domestic product is not growing nearly as fast as our Asian competitors.

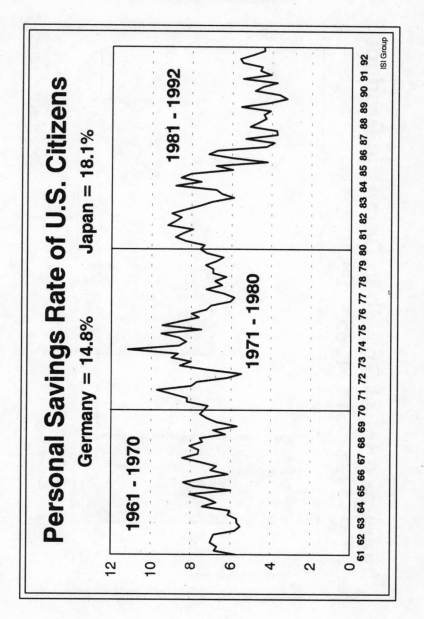

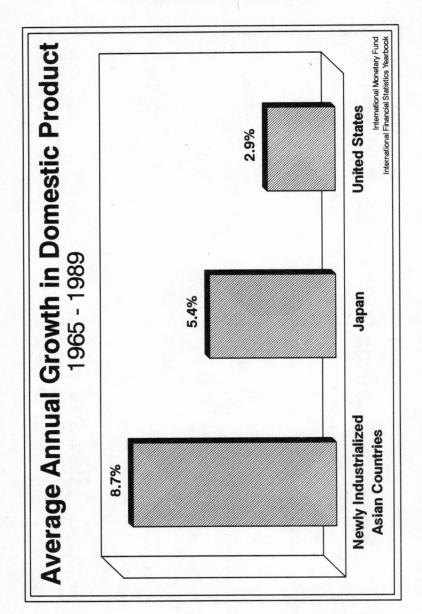

Average Annual Growth in Domestic Product
1965 - 1989

8.7%
Newly Industrialized
Asian Countries

5.4%
Japan

2.9%
United States

International Monetary Fund
International Financial Statistics Yearbook

# UNDER THE HOOD

The gross domestic product of the United States is growing at 2.9% per year while Japan's gross domestic product is growing at an annual rate of about 5.4%. The newly industrialized Asian countries are growing at 8.7%! These are countries like Thailand that we used to think were just interesting places to look at in *National Geographic*. These countries are really growing, and a huge amount of manufacturing is being done there. Some of the manufacturing being done there used to be done right here in the United States. You don't have to like the fact that we live in a tiny world, but I'm telling you we're stuck with it. Somebody wins and somebody loses. Right now, our great country is losing.

## It Didn't Trickle

It's going to take a while to determine the winners and losers in the international arena. However, there's not much doubt as to who won and who lost the trickle-down economics contest of the 1980s. It wasn't even close — the richest 20% of the families won and the other 80% lost.

The graph on page 70 indicates that the richest 20% of the families in the United States received 50% of the total income in 1990, whereas they had received about 45% of the total in 1980. Everyone else dropped 1% from the percentage of income they had received in 1980. Once again, trickle-down economics didn't trickle.

The income in the graph on page 70 was before income tax. You say, "Maybe, the change in after-tax income was a little more equitable." It wasn't. The graph on page 71 shows that after adjusting for inflation, the poorest

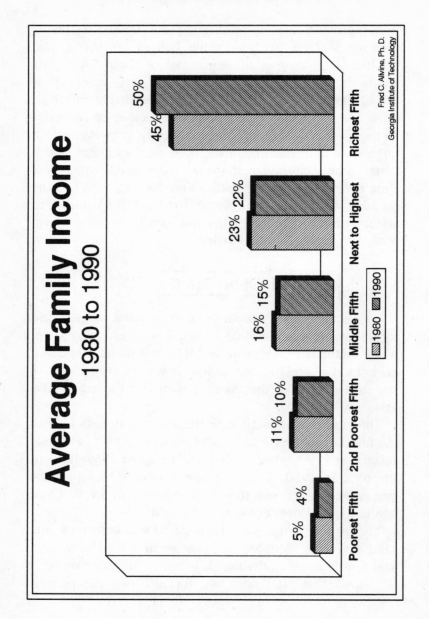

Average Family Income
1980 to 1990

Poorest Fifth — 5% / 4%
2nd Poorest Fifth — 11% / 10%
Middle Fifth — 16% / 15%
Next to Highest — 23% / 22%
Richest Fifth — 45% / 50%

1980  1990

Fred C. Allvine, Ph. D.
Georgia Institute of Technology

70

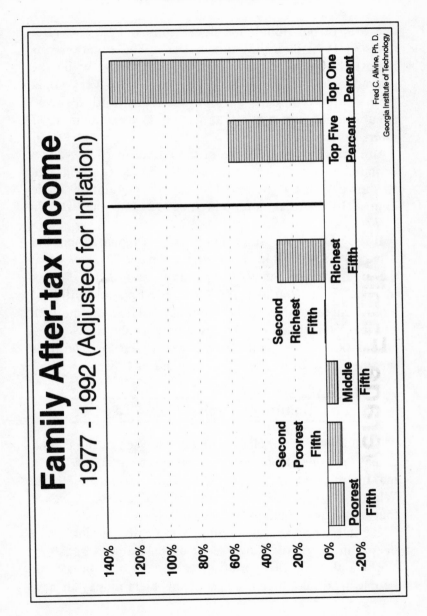

one-fifth of our population netted almost 10% less after taxes in 1992 than they did in 1977. The situation was almost the same for the next two segments, while the second richest fifth of the population had a very slight gain. As you've already guessed, the richest fifth received a substantial increase — almost 30% over their 1977 after-tax earnings.

But the grossest example of the failure of trickle-down economics is the bar on the right-hand side of the graph. It shows that the richest 1% of our population made almost 140% more after tax in 1992 than they did in 1977.

If the income tax structure didn't help the situation, did it hurt it? You decide. The graph on page 73 shows that the poorest fifth of the population had a 16.7% tax increase from 1980 to 1990. The second poorest fifth had a 6.9% increase during the same period. The middle fifth had a 1.2% increase. No surprise here — the richest 40% of our population paid out a lower percentage of their income for taxes in 1990 than they did in 1980.

## Distribution of Capital Gains Tax Cut

Take a look at the chart on page 74. We cut the capital gains tax rate from a maximum rate of 35% to a maximum rate that got as low as 20% during the 1980s. Who got the benefit? The rich did, of course, because that's who owns most of the capital assets.

Capital gains is too lengthy a topic to get into very deeply in this book. However, I do have one suggestion. We should consider offering a special tax break for people who take a risk by investing their money in new

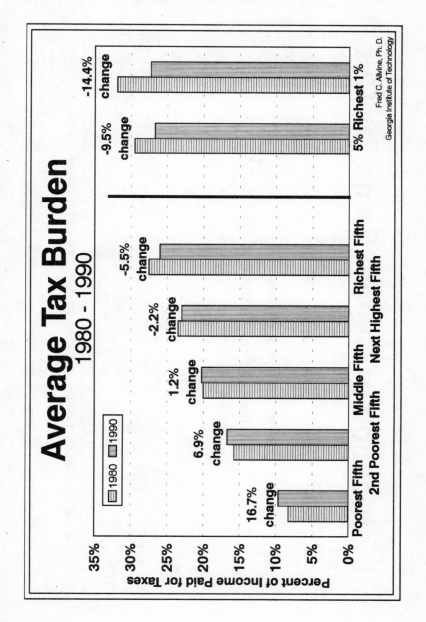

## Average Tax Burden
### 1980 - 1990

□ 1980   ▨ 1990

**Percent of Income Paid for Taxes**

35%  30%  25%  20%  15%  10%  5%  0%

Poorest Fifth

16.7% change

2nd Poorest Fifth

6.9% change

Middle Fifth

1.2% change

Next Highest Fifth

-2.2% change

Richest Fifth

-5.5% change

5% Richest 1%

-9.5% change

-14.4% change

Fred C. Allvine, Ph. D.
Georgia Institute of Technology

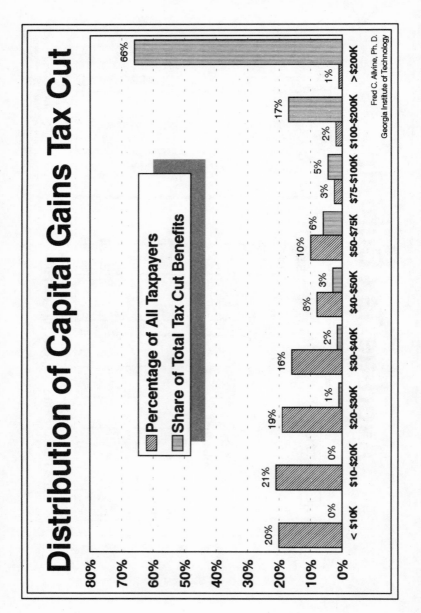

Distribution of Capital Gains Tax Cut

Fred C. Allvine, Ph. D.
Georgia Institute of Technology

businesses. If the money goes into the treasury of a start-up company to build that company, the investor ought to get a tax break for taking a substantial risk. If someone is just shooting dice on Wall Street, we shouldn't offer him or her a tax advantage to do it.

## The Road to a Two-class Society

A disturbing trend has emerged from the decade of greed, the era of trickle-down economics, and the period of capital gains tax manipulation — we are headed for a two-class society. In 1959, the top 4% of U.S. wage earners combined made as much as the bottom 35% of the wage earners combined. In 1989, the top 4% of the wage earners combined made as much as the bottom 51% of the wage earners combined. If this trend indicates an erosion of the middle class, then we are really headed for an economic calamity.

The reason is that the middle class provides the largest portion of our tax revenue. Without a plentiful supply of good-paying jobs, we will lose the backbone of our country — the middle class. We must do everything we can to protect our existing job base, and develop new industries to provide even more good-paying jobs. We should not rest until we have exhausted our supply of workers.

In addition to the factors mentioned above that contribute to the rise of a two-class society, I also suspect this trend is related to the enormous compensation paid to the upper management of some publicly owned companies. The graph on page 76 shows how the salary levels of CEOs in large corporations in

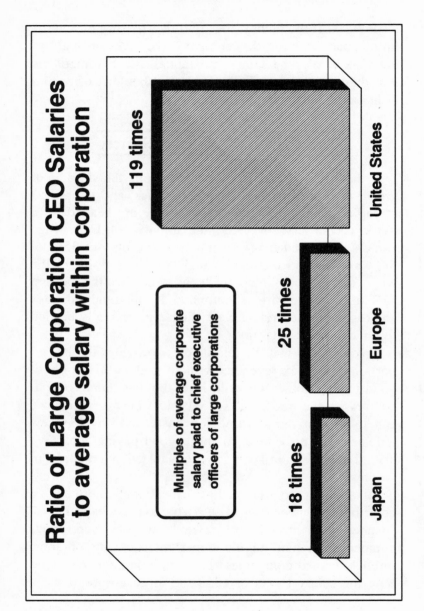

Ratio of Large Corporation CEO Salaries to average salary within corporation

Multiples of average corporate salary paid to chief executive officers of large corporations

119 times — United States

25 times — Europe

18 times — Japan

Japan, Europe, and the United States compare with their employees' average compensation.

In Japan, the upper level managers earn about eighteen times more than the average Japanese worker. In Germany, it's about twenty-five times more. In the United States, the upper level managers in our largest corporations get paid almost 120 times more than the average American worker earns.

Theoretically, the compensation of most upper level management in U.S. companies is tied to the performance of their company. In some cases, bonuses get paid even though the company didn't have a good year. In fact, bonuses may be paid to managers even in years when their companies were badly beaten by overseas competition. That's not good for the companies; that's not good for the stockholders; and that's not good for the country. It may be time for board members to exercise a lot more discretion when determining compensation for the managers of our domestic companies.

If these management guys want to make the really big bucks, they need to be TV anchormen, basketball players, or rock stars. Overpaying company executives damages morale and splits the team. Our overseas competitors understand this.

## It Just Keeps Growing

For the past several charts, we've focused mainly on what has happened within the private sector. We've talked about wages, employment, and taxes. Let's take a look at what has been happening in the public sector.

# NOT FOR SALE AT ANY PRICE

The chart on page 79 shows the annualized growth rates of various agencies within our government from 1950 to 1991. There are some fairly predictable patterns here. Starting at the bottom, the Department of Health and Human Services has grown the most, and the Social Security Administration is a close second. If you ran a business, you'd love to see your work force growing at a 10% - 12% rate year-in and year-out for forty years. You'd really be doing something right. Unfortunately, I'm not certain we can afford to be as enthusiastic about the growth of these agencies. In case you've forgotten, check the graph on page 31 to recall where the largest portion of our money goes each year. It goes to Medicare, Medicaid, Social Security, and other social programs.

Near the top, with very little growth, is Agriculture. At one time, 25% of our people were farmers. Today it's down to 2%, and yet we've still increased the number of people working in the Agriculture Department. A secretary of one of the federal agencies (not Agriculture) told me a story not long ago about a guy who was walking through the Agriculture Department one day. He saw an employee crying at his desk. "What's the matter?" the visitor asked. The man looked up and replied, "My farmer died."

Our government is poorly run and it's poorly managed. There are no villains. It's just that we send people to Washington who don't understand how to get things done, and who don't understand business. They go with a different purpose in life, whatever it might be. But they certainly don't understand business, and they don't understand numbers. In any publicly owned company, you would be put in jail for letting things get this far out of control.

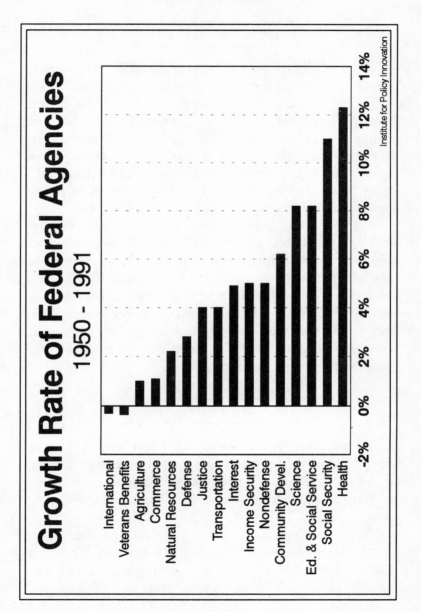

# NOT FOR SALE AT ANY PRICE

## Guns versus Butter

This next chart on page 81 really put our domestic spending in perspective. First, think back to the display of military force that we witnessed in Operation Desert Storm. The price tag for that adventure was about $55 billion. How much did it cost us to watch that smart-bomb sail through the front door of an Iraqi ammo dump, before blowing everything to smithereens? I'm not sure I want to know. One thing is for certain though, we paid for a front row seat, and we got to watch the action.

After considering the amount that we spent on defense in 1992 ($298 billion), it's difficult to imagine that we could be spending almost three times as much at home — not including interest expense on the debt. If we had a perfect society, or even something close, then all the money spent to get it might be tolerable. But compared to the return on our military spending, our domestic spending bought a luxury suite at the Super Bowl, and then the game was canceled.

## 1991 Military Spending

Assume that you're an entrepreneur and you have developed a product that was far superior to anything like it in the marketplace. It cost you a fortune to manufacture it. What would you do with it? You would try to sell it, of course.

Now assume that you're a well-financed benevolent organization that happens to own this product. There are those who would like to have your product, but who cannot afford it. What would you do? You would

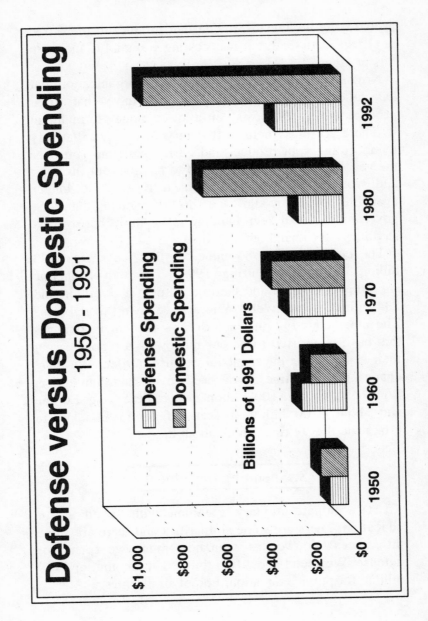

Defense versus Domestic Spending
1950 - 1991

Defense Spending
Domestic Spending

Billions of 1991 Dollars

1950    1960    1970    1980    1992

$1,000   $800   $600   $400   $200   $0

probably be willing to provide that product to them free of charge even though it was costing you a lot to maintain this product.

Now assume that you're a benevolent organization that has fallen on hard times. You still have that great product, and it still costs you a lot of money to maintain it. There are those better off than you who got that way by accepting your product and other gifts from you over the years. They have gotten used to having your product, and would miss it a great deal if it were no longer available. What would you do? If you're the U.S. government, you'd keep handing it out until there wasn't anything left to hand out.

The chart on page 83 indicates that we spent $273 billion on defense during 1991. The two economic superpowers, Japan and Germany, spent $33 billion and $34 billion, respectively. Who are we trying to impress? The other countries that are rich — the other countries that have what used to be our money — are not bearing their share of the international defense burden. We must change that situation. They need to do their fair share. We spend about $100 billion a year defending Europe and about $100 billion a year defending Asia. We're broke and they're rich. Think about it.

## U. S. Spending on Education

Let's compare military spending with spending for education. There are some similarities and there are some differences. You've just seen how much we spend for defense. We spend about two-thirds that amount, or $199 billion, for public education. End of similarities.

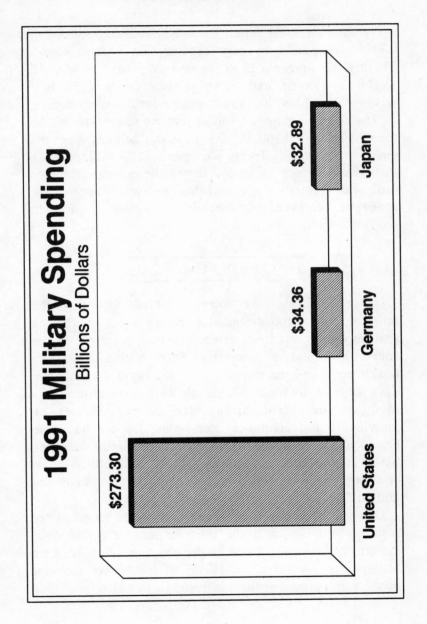

**1991 Military Spending**
Billions of Dollars

$273.30 — United States

$34.36 — Germany

$32.89 — Japan

# NOT FOR SALE AT ANY PRICE

We have the most expertly trained, well-respected, and highly disciplined military organization in the world. There is no longer a close second. We have paid for a world-class outfit, and we've got one to show for it. I wish we could say the same for our educational system.

The chart on page 85 shows that we spent $16 billion for education in 1960. At that time our schools were the envy of the world. Today we spend $199 billion, more than twelve times as much, across the country, and we rank at the bottom of the industrialized world in terms of academic achievement. Throwing money at a problem won't necessarily fix it.

## U. S. Health Care Costs

If you think that we spend a lot of money on the military system and the educational system, you haven't seen anything yet. Look at the chart on page 86. We're spending a total of more than $800 billion a year on health care, and the amount is rising rapidly each year. This amount includes all health care expenditures — Medicare and Medicaid, as well as expenditures by individuals and insurance companies. Do we have the best health care in the world? No. Thirty-four countries have longer life expectancy rates, and thirty-seven countries have lower infant mortality rates than the United States.

Do other countries spend more than we do to get better results? No. We have the most expensive health care system in the world. Look at the chart on page 87. Our health care system takes 12.1% of our gross national product and produces the non-results I just gave you. Our

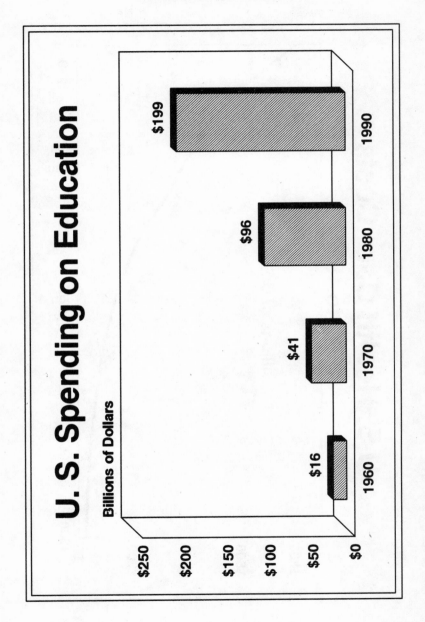

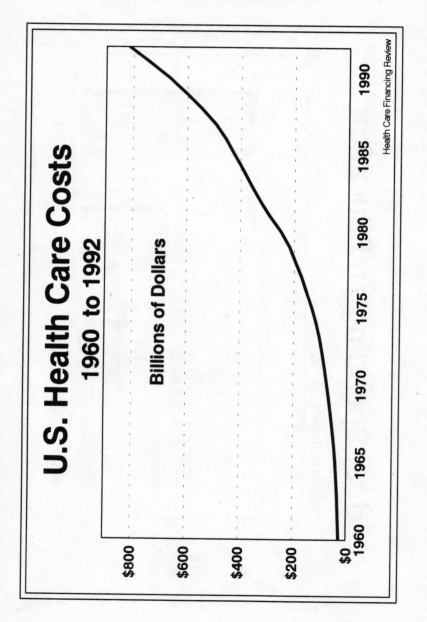

U.S. Health Care Costs
1960 to 1992

Billions of Dollars

Health Care Financing Review

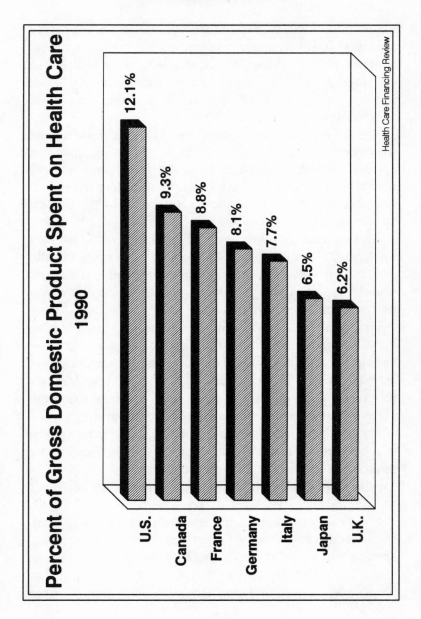

Percent of Gross Domestic Product Spent on Health Care
1990

| Country | Percent |
|---------|---------|
| U.S. | 12.1% |
| Canada | 9.3% |
| France | 8.8% |
| Germany | 8.1% |
| Italy | 7.7% |
| Japan | 6.5% |
| U.K. | 6.2% |

Health Care Financing Review

industrial competitors spend less. Some of them provide universal health care for much less than we're spending. More than thirty million of our people have no health care coverage at all. This is absolute mismanagement of your money and a lack of leadership by the people in Washington.

The Clinton administration has chosen to tackle an overwhelming task — the reform of the health care system. The President has correctly noted that without reform to this area, we have no hope of getting the deficit under control because of the large portion of the federal budget devoted to Medicare and Medicaid.

Although his plan has not yet been finalized, it appears to be very ambitious. To be successful and economically efficient at the same time, it must accomplish several objectives — some of which appear to conflict with current trends and human nature.

For example, one objective of any health care program must be to gain control of spiraling costs — not only reducing the rate of increase, but lowering the absolute cost as well. Yet, another objective of the Administration's program will be to place thirty million Americans into the system who are not now covered by any program.

Another goal that the current participants in the system will certainly demand is that their level of service not be reduced. But, without an increase in personnel to provide for the additional thirty million participants, it is difficult to imagine how the level of service can be maintained. The only way to increase the level of personnel will be to spend additional money to get the service. Of course, spending more money conflicts with the goal of reducing costs. I'm not saying that a solution can't be found or that we shouldn't try to find one. I'm only saying that whoever solves this problem, will rank up there with Edison, Ford, and the Wright Brothers.

We must be careful with the implementation of any health care reform program. The stakes are too high, and the consequences are too important. We must run pilot studies of any proposals.

## Our Most Precious Resource

We are blessed with many natural resources in this country. But the most precious resource of all is our children. Their welfare is the rightful objective of many of the programs on which we spend so much money — namely education and health care. So why don't we see better results? For one reason, it's the environment in which these children live.

The chart on page 90 shows another disturbing trend that we must solve. In 1970, 14% of our children lived in poverty. Today we have 21% — more than one out of five — of our children living in poverty. We will never be able to solve the dropout and discipline problems in our schools until we can get our children into a situation where they have at least some kind of minimum standard of supervision and attention at home.

Where does the rest of the world stand in terms of child poverty rates? I'm embarrassed to have you look at the chart on page 91. The rest of the industrialized world has lower poverty rates than we do.

Let's assume you're still not convinced that this problem needs to be corrected as quickly as possible. I ask you to look at your children and grandchildren — the people you love the most in the world and would literally

U. S. Child Poverty Rates
1970 to 1991

Institute for Policy Innovation

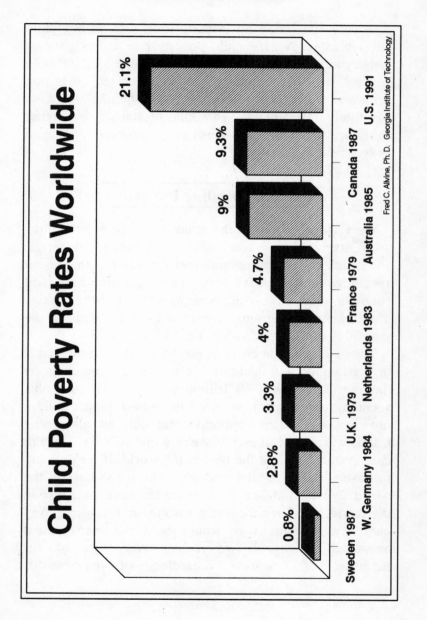

Child Poverty Rates Worldwide

Sweden 1987 — 0.8%
W. Germany 1984 — 2.8%
U.K. 1979 — 3.3%
Netherlands 1983 — 4%
France 1979 — 4.7%
Australia 1985 — 9%
Canada 1987 — 9.3%
U.S. 1991 — 21.1%

Fred C. Allwine, Ph. D.  Georgia Institute of Technology

91

give your life for in an instant. Then look at our child poverty rates. A 21% child poverty rate in the greatest country in the history of man is unthinkable. A 21% child poverty rate in a country whose alabaster cities are supposed to gleam undimmed by human tears is absolutely unacceptable. This kind of statistic is another alarming indicator of where an improperly managed government has taken us.

## Federal Spending Projection

We've touched on all the major areas of expenditures — entitlement programs, military spending, education, and health care. Let's assume that we stay on our present spending course, have no major catastrophes, and continue to offer the same benefits to future beneficiaries of entitlement programs. Where does that put us in the year 2020? In Deep Voodoo, I'm afraid

Take a look at the chart on page 93. The current trends in Washington will lead to projected federal spending, by the year 2020, of $3.9 trillion per year. To fund this spending requirement, we need to do two things: build a growing, expanding economy; and cut out all of the fraud, waste, and abuse. If we're going to have a health care system, make it the best in the world. If we're going to have a public school system, make it the best in the world. We can't afford to pay more than everyone else in the world, and have the worst systems in the world. Any company run this way would hold the management accountable. Instead, we reelect over 90% of our members of Congress regardless of the results.

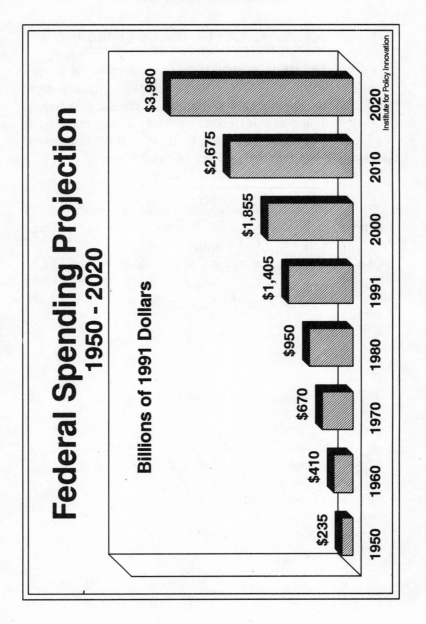

Federal Spending Projection
1950 - 2020

Billions of 1991 Dollars

Institute for Policy Innovation

| Year | Amount |
|------|--------|
| 1950 | $235 |
| 1960 | $410 |
| 1970 | $670 |
| 1980 | $950 |
| 1991 | $1,405 |
| 2000 | $1,855 |
| 2010 | $2,675 |
| 2020 | $3,980 |

# NOT FOR SALE AT ANY PRICE

## Mortgaging Our Children's Future

Passing the American Dream on to our children is very important to all of us. When I was a young man, it took less than two generations to double the standard of living. Today, because of the mismanagement of our country, it will take twelve generations to double the standard of living. We have mortgaged our children's future.

Can we fix this? Yes.

Will it be easy? No.

But, the challenge will be a whole lot easier for us than the people who came before us in terms of what they had to do to create this great country.

I'm not suggesting that we put our lives on the line in an effort to win an economic war. But I am suggesting that we work together to solve these problems. We'll see how in the next chapter.

# Chapter Three

## Let's Fix It

There was more bad news in the last chapter than you ever wanted to think about. The good news is that all of these problems can be solved. It will take some hard work and firm determination to make it happen, but it can be done.

After looking at the following quotation, I think we can immediately come to the conclusion that history does, in fact, repeat itself.

> *The budget should be balanced.*
> *The treasury should be refilled.*
> *Public debt should be reduced.*
> *The arrogance of public officials*
> *should be controlled.*

Although Cicero spoke these words over 2,000 years ago, they certainly apply to our country today. Let's start where Cicero started, and talk about balancing the budget.

# NOT FOR SALE AT ANY PRICE

## Balancing the Budget

We need to balance the federal budget for the same reasons that you have to balance your personal budget. The banker may let you borrow for a little while, but one day you'll reach your limit. Our country may one day reach the limit with its bankers, who are primarily pension funds, mutual funds, and foreign countries. Our debt and interest payments could get so high that our creditors might believe we can no longer avoid the alternative of printing money without value to get us out of the problem.

Take a look at the graph on page 97. The top line of the chart is a 1992 estimate by the Congressional Budget Office of how much the annual deficits will run through 1998. They are anywhere between $190 billion and $255 billion a year. The lower line is an estimate of what the deficits would be under a plan that I proposed during 1992. That plan called for a reduction in the deficit of $754 billion over a five-year period. My plan would even give us a small budget surplus in 1998. This does not mean that we would have paid off our $4 trillion debt. It just means that we would have turned things around to the point that we could begin to pay off the debt by using the annual surplus. We'll take a look at that plan in a moment.

The decision we need to make is whether we're going to ignore this ticking time bomb and continue to go one billion dollars deeper into debt every working day, or whether we should get on with the business of paying our bills and creating jobs.

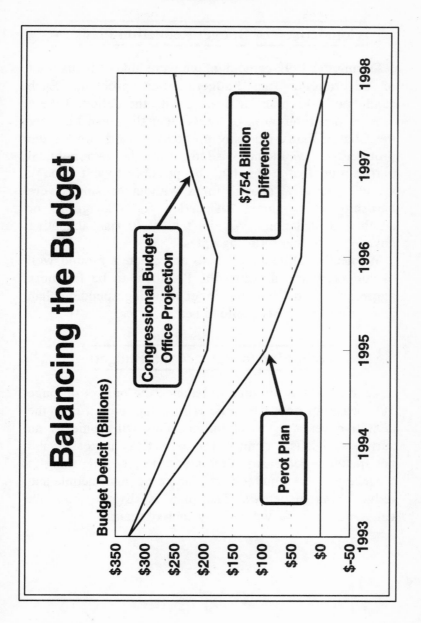

## Comparison of Budget Reduction Plans

During the 1992 campaign, we were able to focus a lot of attention on the budget deficit problem. Each candidate had a plan for dealing with the deficit. Take a look at the graph on page 99. Neither the Bush Plan nor the Clinton Plan made any progress toward solving the problem. Conventional wisdom from the two political parties said that it wouldn't be possible to cut enough spending or raise enough taxes without causing severe hardship or economic dislocation for one group or another. Translation: "We don't want to risk alienating anyone out of fear of losing votes."

We need to build a consensus and create a groundswell of support that will allow the President to be far more aggressive with Congress about reducing spending than any president has been able to be.

## Perot Plan to Balance the Budget

Take a look at my plan to balance the budget on page 100. It shows how we could reduce the budget over the next five years by $754 billion. This will come as no surprise — it is a combination of net tax increases and net spending decreases. You would do the same thing to balance your own budget: try to increase your income and reduce your expenses. The plan is divided into six categories, and we will discuss each of them.

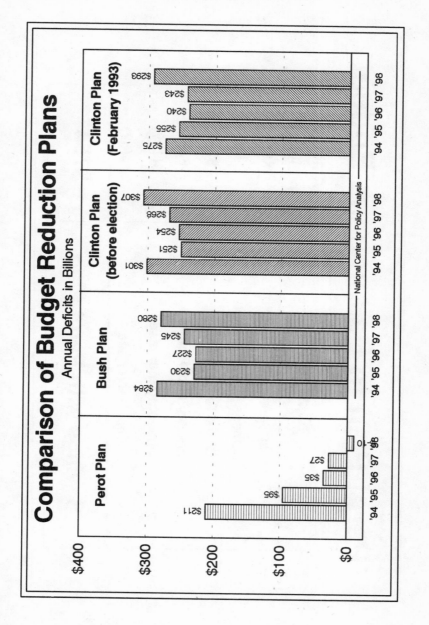

**Comparison of Budget Reduction Plans**
Annual Deficits in Billions

National Center for Policy Analysis

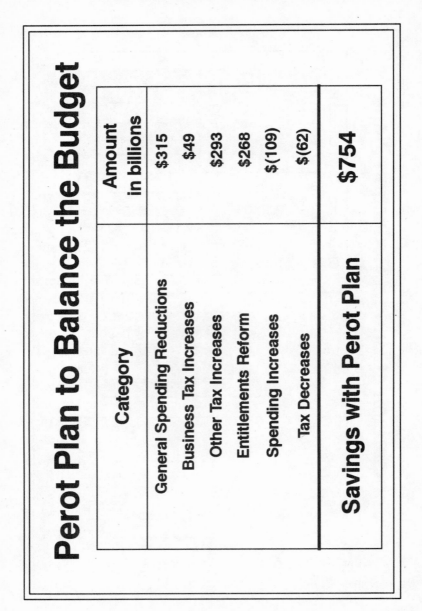

# Perot Plan to Balance the Budget

| Category | Amount in billions |
|---|---|
| General Spending Reductions | $315 |
| Business Tax Increases | $49 |
| Other Tax Increases | $293 |
| Entitlements Reform | $268 |
| Spending Increases | $(109) |
| Tax Decreases | $(62) |
| **Savings with Perot Plan** | **$754** |

# LET'S FIX IT

## General Spending Reductions

Take a look at the chart on page 102. I proposed cutting general spending by $315 billion over the five-year period. General spending includes all areas of government, other than the entitlement programs, which we'll discuss in a moment.

I proposed a 15% cut in discretionary programs over five years that would be accomplished with two steps. First, save $35 billion, or 5%, by cutting specific programs that are unnecessary or no longer needed. Then, make an across-the-board cut of another 10% in the budgets of all departments, which will save $73 billion.

The defense budget can be cut by $40 billion over the five-year period. Nothing is more important than the security of our country. But our well-being now depends as much on *economic* security as on *military* security. We have the necessary troops and weapons ready to confront any serious threats to our national interests. We need to focus on the economic threat to our future.

Numerous programs that amount to little more than subsidies for business have found their way into the budget over the years. We should eliminate these subsidies where there is no longer a legitimate reason for them. A good example is subsidies paid to huge agricultural corporations. We can save $22 billion over the five-year period by cutting subsidies to business.

Finally, the biggest cut in the general spending area will be absolutely painless. We can reduce the amount of interest we pay on the debt by $145 billion over the five-year period because we won't have to borrow as much money during that time.

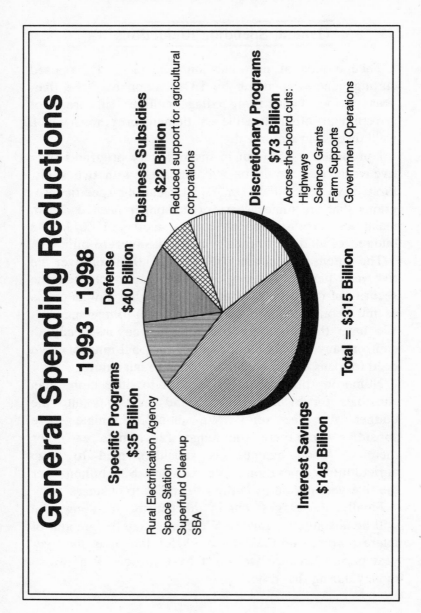

General Spending Reductions
1993 - 1998

Specific Programs
$35 Billion

Rural Electrification Agency
Space Station
Superfund Cleanup
SBA

Defense
$40 Billion

Business Subsidies
$22 Billion

Reduced support for agricultural corporations

Discretionary Programs
$73 Billion

Across-the-board cuts:

Highways
Science Grants
Farm Supports
Government Operations

Interest Savings
$145 Billion

Total = $315 Billion

# LET'S FIX IT

## Business Tax Increases

Here is another measure that will be painless. Take a look at the graph on page 104. We need to improve the collection of taxes from foreign corporations doing business in the United States. As it stands now, we might as well send invitations to set up operations in this country. Actually, through the help of their Washington lobbyists, foreign companies often write their own invitations. We can pick up an additional $21 billion by improving the collection of taxes from foreign-owned companies doing business here.

We can save $16 billion a year by reducing the business entertainment deduction from 80% of the cost for entertainment to 50% of the cost. If you're talking to a potential customer in a restaurant, why should Uncle Sam let you take a deduction for what you just ate when you could have had the same conversation in your office or in your customer's office without eating? We should be selling our ability to perform, not our capacity to do lunch.

We can bring in an extra $12 billion by increasing certain user fees and imposing new user fees for many of the assets and services now provided by the federal government, such as the inland waterways and air traffic control services. We shouldn't be reluctant to charge a fair price for these items simply because we haven't done so in the past.

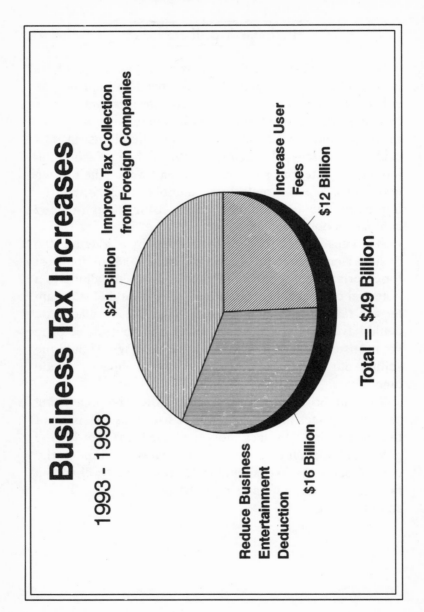

# LET'S FIX IT

## Other Tax Increases

Another set of tax increases is shown on page 106. Each of them would impact individuals, and some of the increases would fall on businesses, as well.

The most controversial tax proposal is the gas tax increase of 10¢ per gallon, per year, for five years, amounting to an increase of 50¢ or a total tax of 85¢ per gallon in 1998. This would raise an additional $158 billion. As our domestic oil reserves decline, we are becoming more dependent on foreign supplies. A higher gas tax won't eliminate this foreign dependency, but it will slow down the rate of increase in our dependency.

The tobacco tax increase would bring in $19 billion and help offset the subsidies we pay farmers to grow tobacco. You might want to read that last sentence again. This is an absurd situation. Because of the power of the tobacco lobby and its influence over some key senators and members of the House, a portion of your tax money actually pays for growing tobacco.

The federal government might as well increase the cigarette tax because it looks like the states will do it anyway. Massachusetts recently raised their tax from 26¢ to 51¢ per pack. Smoking kills 400,000 people every year, from lung cancer to emphysema to heart attacks. We pay billions of dollars in medical costs each year for smoking-related diseases. The surgeon general recently released a report indicating that in addition to the risk of disease smokers bring on themselves, secondary smoke can cause lung cancer in non-smokers. Smoking is absolutely ludicrous, and we should do everything we can to help people kick the habit.

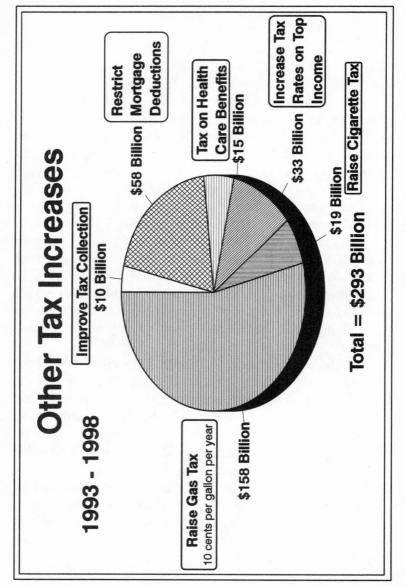

Other Tax Increases

1993 - 1998

Improve Tax Collection
$10 Billion

Restrict Mortgage Deductions
$58 Billion

Tax on Health Care Benefits
$15 Billion

Increase Tax Rates on Top Income
$33 Billion

$19 Billion  Raise Cigarette Tax

Total = $293 Billion

Raise Gas Tax
10 cents per gallon per year
$158 Billion

# LET'S FIX IT

We can improve our tax collection methods and bring in an additional $10 billion. This would require updating the systems used by the Internal Revenue Service, but the investment would pay for itself almost overnight. It has been estimated by former presidential candidate Michael Dukakis that improved methods of tax collection might actually bring in an additional $50 billion to $100 billion a year, so $10 billion seems feasible.

We need to collect more income taxes from those who can afford to pay. I proposed an increase in the top marginal rate from 31% to 33% with the possibility of raising the rate to 35% if we can't get enough revenue from other sources. Raising the rate on the top income level will bring in $33 billion over the next five years.

Finally, I proposed two other changes affecting individuals. I would limit the mortgage interest expense deduction to mortgages under $250,000 on a taxpayer's principal residence. Currently, if you have a vacation home, you may be able to deduct that interest, also. For example, if the mortgages on your principal residence plus your vacation home total less than $1 million, then you can now deduct the interest on the vacation home mortgage. Do we really need to give someone a tax break for using a vacation home? We don't encourage people to take vacations by giving them tax breaks for staying in hotels. The other change affecting individuals is to tax the cost of employer-provided health care programs in excess of a premium of $135 per month for an individual and $335 per month for a family.

## Reform of Entitlement Programs

As we have already seen, entitlement programs account for the largest single portion of government expenditures. If we're going to make any substantial cuts in government spending, then some of the spending will have to be cut from these programs. But, I think we can do it in a manner that will cause very little hardship.

Take a look at the graph on page 109. The second largest savings of the entire deficit reduction plan, behind interest on the debt, can be achieved by instituting health care cost containment procedures. This would save $141 billion over five years.

We have already seen the reason why we can hope to achieve this savings. We are spending far more on health care than the rest of the world, and we don't even have the best system to show for it. After we've had a chance to reform our health care system, we should see some dramatic savings in the Medicare and Medicaid programs.

We need to repeal the salary cap on Medicare premiums. Currently, an individual stops paying the Medicare insurance premium of 1.45% when his or her salary exceeds $135,000. Under my proposal, the Medicare premium would be paid on all salary, wages, and self-employment income. We would collect an additional $29 billion with this measure.

Most Social Security recipients elect to take advantage of Medicare Part B, which is the hospitalization portion of the insurance coverage. They are charged a monthly premium that is deducted from their Social Security check. This premium was originally supposed to cover

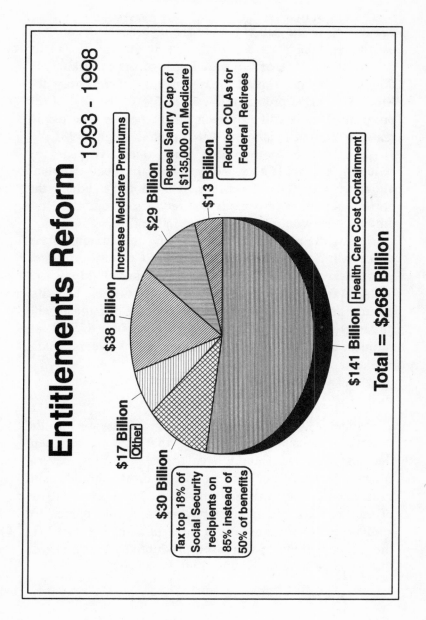

## Entitlements Reform
### 1993 - 1998

Increase Medicare Premiums

$38 Billion

$29 Billion

Repeal Salary Cap of $135,000 on Medicare

$13 Billion

Reduce COLAs for Federal Retirees

$17 Billion Other

$30 Billion

Tax top 18% of Social Security recipients on 85% instead of 50% of benefits

$141 Billion Health Care Cost Containment

Total = $268 Billion

NOT FOR SALE AT ANY PRICE

about 50% of the actual cost of the insurance. Because of escalating health care costs, this premium now only covers about 25% of the actual cost of the program. My deficit reduction plan recommends increasing the Medicare Part B premium to cover 35% of the cost of the program. This is still a bargain for the people who use it, and it will bring in an extra $38 billion through 1998.

We can save another $13 billion over five years by reducing the scheduled increases of the cost-of-living-allowances to federal retirees. This doesn't reduce the current benefit of anyone; it just reduces by one-third the amount they would have received in the future.

Finally, the plan calls for increasing the amount of tax on certain Social Security recipients. Currently, retirees who make over $25,000 per year as individuals, or $32,000 filing jointly, pay taxes on 50% of their benefits. Taxing an additional 35% of the benefits for those who already pay taxes will only affect about 18% of all retirees, but it will raise $30 billion over five years.

## Spending Increases

We need to start treating money like water in the desert. Any additional money that the government decides to spend should have to pass through several filters. The first filter is that an expenditure should result in new jobs. But most government expenditures, outside of entitlements and interest payments, result in jobs for somebody. So we must run it through another filter. Will the job contribute to increased productivity and make us more competitive in the world marketplace?

# LET'S FIX IT

The chart on page 112 indicates that we need to spend $46 billion on additional research and development programs. This investment can pay huge dividends in terms of new products and industries that can be created from yet-to-be-discovered technologies.

We need to spend an additional $40 billion repairing our infrastructure — roads, bridges, and tunnels. We have an enormous investment in these valuable assets that we cannot continue to let deteriorate. An efficient transportation system may be the most important factor affecting our worker productivity. Our workers can't do much if they're sitting in traffic.

We need to allocate an additional $12 billion to education. This is not a large amount in relation to these other spending increases, but as I said earlier, just throwing money at a problem is not going to solve it.

We need to transfer an additional $11 billion to our cities. It is important that we do as much as we can to save our cities.

## Tax Decreases

Because a tax decrease affects the budget in the same manner as a spending increase, we should apply the same filters I mentioned above. All of the tax decreases shown in the chart on page 113 are designed to stimulate jobs and business.

We need to give a tax credit to businesses for training workers. Because of the displacement that will occur as we shift away from our past emphasis on the military, it will be necessary to retrain our former military personnel and civilian workers in defense-related industries. This

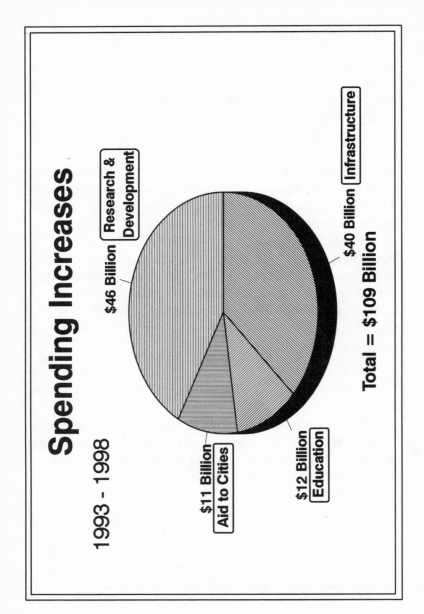

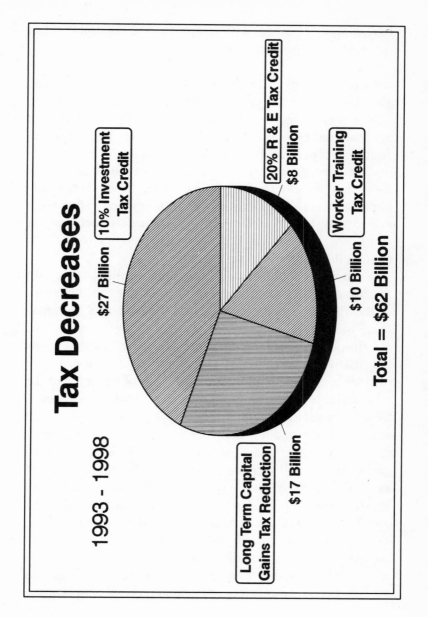

retraining tax credit will result in $10 billion of lost revenue to the government.

The investment tax credit should be reinstated to stimulate industrial investment in plant and equipment. This investment tax credit will reduce the tax income by $27 billion. One of the reasons we fell behind our international competitors is that we let our buildings and equipment deteriorate without adequate provision for replacement. Our corporations paid out dividends when they should have been putting aside funds for future improvements. The factories of Germany and Japan were ruined in World War II. After we built new factories for them, we watched as they out-produced us from their new facilities. Pretty simple, isn't it.

My proposed plan would give an $8 billion tax credit for research and experimentation to target the industries of the future to make certain that we lead and dominate those industries.

I proposed a reduction in the long-term capital gains rate that would reduce tax revenue by $17 billion. It will provide a mechanism to get an infusion of money into the treasuries of companies, preferably small companies. Small companies can create more jobs more quickly than any other method of investment. But this is high-risk money. Investors may lose their money, so the capital gains tax cut will provide an incentive for them to invest as opposed to buying government bonds or federally insured bank certificates of deposit. Believe me, this tax credit money will come back again, and again, and again. The small amount of money that goes into these companies and the small amount of taxes that we don't collect will be more than offset by the payroll taxes and income taxes coming from the thousands of people these companies may eventually employ. It will be a giant financial pump for our country.

In my opinion, a tax reduction package similar to the one outlined here could prove to be the most efficient means of stimulating the economy that we could devise. The reason is that this tax credit will not be a free ride for business. They will have to undertake some risk because they will have to invest real dollars. This could be the beginning of an intelligent, supportive relationship between business and government.

## It All Adds Up

The two charts on pages 116 and 117 take everything we have talked about in the six categories and shows the details. It may be more than you'd care to look through, but it's all there.

No one is claiming this is a perfect solution to the problem of dealing with the budget deficit. The point is that it is at least *an* idea of how to get to a balanced budget in a reasonable amount of time. Let's assume the administration and Congress find the will to implement a plan like mine. If, in six months, somebody has a better idea or if something isn't working, that's fine — change the plan. It won't be carved into the side of a building. The thing we cannot do is just sit around playing Lawrence Welk music thinking everything is "wannaful, wannaful, wannaful." We must get to work.

# Perot Deficit Reduction Plan

(Billions of Dollars)

*(Note: a positive amount indicates a reduction in the deficit)*

| | 1994 | 1995 | 1996 | 1997 | 1998 | Total |
|---|---|---|---|---|---|---|
| **DEFENSE SPENDING** | | | | | | |
| Additional annual 1.6% real reduction | 1.1 | 3.6 | 6.8 | 11.4 | 17.1 | 40.0 * |
| **DOMESTIC DISCRETIONARY SPENDING** | | | | | | |
| Cuts | | | | | | |
| Programs cuts (5%) | 3.0 | 5.5 | 7.5 | 9.0 | 10.0 | 35.0 |
| Across-the-board Administrative cut (10%) | 5.0 | 10.0 | 15.0 | 20.0 | 23.0 | 73.0 |
| Increases | | | | | | |
| Increased Research and Development | 0.0 | (4.0) | (9.5) | (15.0) | (17.0) | (45.5) |
| Aid to Cities | (1.7) | (2.1) | (2.4) | (2.6) | (2.8) | (11.6) |
| Education | (3.0) | (2.6) | (2.4) | (2.2) | (2.2) | (12.4) |
| Infrastructure | (8.0) | (8.0) | (8.0) | (8.0) | (8.0) | (40.0) |
| Total Change in Discretionary Spending | (4.7) | (1.2) | 0.2 | 1.2 | 3.0 | (1.5) * |
| **ENTITLEMENT SPENDING** | | | | | | |
| Raise ceiling from 50% to 85% of social security benefits includible as taxable income | 2.8 | 5.8 | 6.4 | 7.1 | 7.9 | 30.0 |
| Limit COLA's to Federal employees for 5 years | 0.6 | 1.5 | 2.6 | 3.6 | 4.7 | 13.0 |
| Repeal cap ($135,000) on Medicare payroll tax | 2.7 | 5.8 | 6.2 | 6.7 | 7.5 | 28.9 |
| Increase Medicare SMI premium from 25% to 35% | 2.8 | 4.0 | 6.0 | 10.1 | 14.8 | 37.7 |
| Medicare cost containment | 3.8 | 9.0 | 15.2 | 23.1 | 31.4 | 82.5 |
| Medicaid cost containment | 2.9 | 6.9 | 11.3 | 16.3 | 21.4 | 58.8 |
| Reduce agricultural supports and tariffs | 0.8 | 2.4 | 2.9 | 4.1 | 6.8 | 17.0 |
| Total Savings from Entitlements Reform | 16.4 | 35.4 | 50.6 | 71.0 | 94.5 | 267.9 * |

# Perot Deficit Reduction Plan
## (Billions of Dollars)

*(Note: a positive amount indicates a reduction in the deficit)*

| | 1994 | 1995 | 1996 | 1992 | 1998 | Total |
|---|---|---|---|---|---|---|
| **TAX REFORMS** | | | | | | |
| Targeted 10% Investment Tax Credit | (5.0) | (5.2) | (5.3) | (5.5) | (5.6) | (26.6) |
| Targeted capital gains tax reduction | 3.8 | (3.5) | (5.9) | (5.8) | (5.4) | (16.8) |
| Permanent extension of 20% R&E tax credit | (0.8) | (1.4) | (1.6) | (1.9) | (2.2) | (7.9) |
| Tax credit for worker training | (1.0) | (1.8) | (2.1) | (2.5) | (2.9) | (10.3) |
| Increase top marginal income tax rate from 31% to 33 | 3.7 | 6.9 | 7.4 | 7.5 | 7.6 | 33.1 |
| Restrict mortgage deductions | 1.1 | 2.8 | 3.2 | 4.1 | 4.6 | 15.8 |
| Tax some employer-paid health insurance benefits | 6.1 | 9.9 | 11.6 | 13.6 | 15.9 | 57.1 |
| Imposition of user fees | 1.8 | 2.4 | 2.5 | 2.6 | 2.7 | 12.0 |
| Elimination of wasteful subsidies | 1.9 | 3.7 | 4.7 | 5.4 | 6.2 | 21.9 |
| Tighten transfer pricing and source rules | 4.0 | 4.2 | 4.3 | 4.4 | 4.5 | 21.4 |
| Restrict business entertainment deductions to 50% | 1.6 | 3.5 | 3.5 | 3.6 | 3.7 | 15.9 |
| Increase excise taxes on tobacco | 3.0 | 4.0 | 3.9 | 3.9 | 3.8 | 18.6 |
| Increase motor fuel tax (10¢ increase per year) | 12.5 | 22.3 | 32.0 | 41.0 | 50.0 | 157.8 |
| Improved tax collection procedures | 1.8 | 2.0 | 2.0 | 2.2 | 2.2 | 10.2 |
| Net Revenue from Tax Reforms | 34.5 | 49.8 | 60.2 | 72.6 | 85.1 | 302.2 * |
| | | | | | | |
| Total Non-Interest Reduction | 47.3 | 87.6 | 117.8 | 156.2 | 199.7 | 608.6 ** |
| Interest Expense Savings from Deficit Reduction | 2.2 | 11.3 | 25.2 | 42.3 | 64.3 | 145.3 |
| **Total Deficit Reduction** (A) | 49.5 | 98.9 | 143.0 | 198.5 | 264.0 | 753.9 |
| | | | | | | |
| Projected Deficits (per Congressional Budget Office) | 260.0 | 194.0 | 178.0 | 226.0 | 254.0 | 1,112.0 |
| | | | | | | |
| Remaining Deficit (A) - (B) | 210.5 | 95.1 | 35.0 | 27.5 | (10.0) | 358.1 |

## Then and Now

During the 1992 campaign, the other candidates acknowledged the need to balance the budget, but neither of their economic plans indicated a serious attempt to make it happen. Take another look at the graph on page 99 for a comparison of the economic plans submitted by the three major candidates. Apparently the other candidates feared the American public would react negatively to a suggestion that the patient was sick and that strong medicine was needed now. My contention is that a dose of strong medicine now is preferable to the major surgery that will be necessary in a few years if we don't take action.

Take a look at the series of bars on the right-hand side of the graph at page 99. This is a revised estimate of the deficits under the blueprint prepared by the President and approved by both the Senate and the House of Representatives. The deficits are somewhat lower than originally projected, but they are still in the same ballpark.

The problem with this proposed budget is that we are going to get hit with immediate tax increases with little likelihood of tax decreases in the coming years. The bulk of the proposed spending cuts won't take effect until two years from now. However, Congress passes a new spending plan every year, so we're not guaranteed that we will ever see the spending cuts that we're paying higher taxes to get. If you throw in the fact that we're still not certain how to pay for a new health care system, then we really have some big question marks.

# Chapter Four

## Good People, Bad System

The American people elect outstanding citizens to serve us in Washington. The system in Washington is the problem — not the people we send there. We must reform the system. The recently proposed reforms are conceptual, like an artist's sketch for a new house. Congress, not the President, will develop the detailed blueprint. Lobbyists' hands will be holding the pencil as the blueprints are drawn. The taxpayers have no voice. The President has asked all of us to hold Washington's feet to the fire to make certain these reforms break through the Washington gridlock and are passed into law. Together we can do it.

Some of the finest people in our Congress are serving on a joint committee formed to review proposals for government reform. This committee — The Joint Committee on the Organization of Congress — is composed of an equal number of Democrats and Republicans. The members of this committee are working to get reforms passed. But we, the owners, must let our senators and representatives know that we want real reform. We must speak louder than the special interests.

## Who Are the Special Interests?

The special interests are comprised of domestic lobbyists, foreign lobbyists, and representatives of political action committees with access to government officials. They specialize in greasing the skids in Washington with money. Lobbying is a growth industry in our country. In 1960, there were less than 400 lobbyists. By 1992, the number had grown to more than 40,000.

How do lobbyists work? They provide millions of dollars for political campaigns. The American people have recently watched news reports showing our members of Congress going to vacation resorts with lobbyists — with the plane tickets, lodging, meals, and all the trimmings paid for by the lobbyists. Shortly after the 1992 election, one of the political parties even had a weekend retreat that was paid for and attended by lobbyists. These lobbyists have just one interest — to pick the taxpayer's pocket. We, the people, not the special interests, own this country.

You might ask just how the taxpayer gets his pocket picked by the foreign lobbyists. Here's an example.

Lobbyists for Japanese truck manufacturers spent $3 million to lobby our representatives in Washington. The problem from the perspective of the Japanese truck manufacturer was a 25% tariff on trucks that were imported into the United States. Foreign automobiles are imported, but the tariff is only 2½%. The higher tariffs on trucks made the Japanese vehicles less competitive and less profitable. The solution was simple they reasoned, "Let's just get the trucks designated as cars." Three million dollars later, their hired lobbyists made it happen.

There was another problem. Cars had to meet higher mileage and pollution emission standards or else the local dealers would incur a penalty when the trucks were sold. Not a problem. The same lobbyists just got the trucks — which were now considered to be cars — designated as trucks once they arrived at the dealers' lots.

This one-time expenditure of $3 million for lobbyists has saved the Japanese truck manufacturers $1.2 billion. It costs us an additional $300 million every year. Hardworking, taxpaying Americans have to bear this $1.2 billion burden that is not being collected from Japanese truck manufacturers. This is wrong.

You might think that anybody this clever is worth meeting. If you are discouraged by the cost of a trip overseas to introduce yourself, don't worry, it won't be necessary. They live right here in the United States — probably in Virginia or Maryland — and most of them used to work for you as government employees. You paid for their training and contacts. They have shipped millions of jobs overseas. In a moment, we'll see how it happened.

If you don't remember anything else from this book, remember this —

WE HAVE PEOPLE GOING TO WASHINGTON
TO CASH IN RATHER THAN TO SERVE.

We have people serving in Congress, the White House, and other agencies for a few years and then leaving. They hire out as foreign lobbyists at salaries of several hundred thousand dollars a year. They are selling influence and access to government officials who can help foreign clients of the lobbyists get what they want — or prevent something from happening to them.

Between 1980 and 1991, 158 former federal officials left office to become registered foreign agents.

Take a look at the list below; it's like looking at a list of AWOL soldiers who turned up fighting for the enemy. This is the reason that two million high-paying factory jobs were shipped to Asia during the 1980s.

- 25 White House officials
- 65 executive agency officials
- 50 Congressional staff members
- 10 members of the House of Representatives
- 8 Senators

THIS IS ECONOMIC TREASON.

We have 35-year-olds making $200,000 to $300,000 a year, who would have trouble finding a minimum-wage job outside Washington, simply because they have that coveted Washington commodity — access. They don't have any skills. All they've done is work for a senior official in Washington or work in presidential campaigns. These former government employees are using their contacts in Washington and foreign money lobbying Congress to make bad trade decisions for the American people. The Americans who have lost their jobs because of these trade agreements were typically making $440 per week. They are now working at lower-paying jobs making approximately $270 per week — if they have a job at all.

Even worse — and I hope you will put your foot down and make both the Democrats and Republicans throw their cards on the table on this one — during 1992 both parties had foreign lobbyists working on the presidential campaigns. That's like having Russian spies in the middle of a presidential campaign during the Cold War. The only thing that has changed is that today it's a business war. This is unacceptable to the people — the owners of this country.

## They Should Know

Our most fundamental problem is that our government is responding to the wrong forces. It is driven by huge sums of money being received from foreign lobbyists and special interests — rather than the will of the American people.

How does the rest of the world look at us as a result of these practices?

The Japanese, in their *Economic Journal* say:

> Influence in Washington is just like
> Indonesia — it's for sale.

Our good friends, the British, in *The Economist* say:

> Washington's culture of influence for hire
> is uniquely open to all buyers, foreign
> and domestic. Its lawful ways of corrupt-
> ing public policy remain unrivaled.

The Dutch writer, Karel van Wolferen, says:

> A big part of the problem is that
> Americans can be bought so easily.

Makes you really proud, doesn't it?

# NOT FOR SALE AT ANY PRICE

Our challenge, as we reform our government, is to erect huge signs that say to the world — **NOT FOR SALE AT ANY PRICE**.

## Mr. Smith Goes to Washington

In September 1991, the Washington *Post* published an article entitled "Mr. Smith Goes to Washington—The Real-Life Sequel." It was written by a first-time candidate for Congress who came to Washington to participate in a workshop hosted by his political party. The purpose was to train candidates on how to run for office. The moderators of the seminar included members of Congress, PAC representatives, pollsters, consultants, and media specialists who told the candidates how the "game" is played. Here are some insights from the Washington "professionals" as to how the political system works.

A party member — "Money drives this town."

Consultant — "You have to sell yourself in Washington first."

Consultant — "The game of raising PAC money here in Washington will make the difference. Understand how the game is played. It's crucial to your being one of the few that will win."

U.S. Congressman — "Raising campaign money from Washington PACs is much easier than from individuals because it's a business relationship."

Party member — "These people [PACs] are paid to give you money. You have to *do* certain things, but they *want* to give you money."

# GOOD PEOPLE, BAD SYSTEM

PAC representative — "I don't give my people's money to those I think are going to lose, so you have to convince me you're going to win."

PAC representative — "When you take PAC money, you are saying you're their friend."

U.S. Congressman — "Some of you may be under pressure to repudiate PACs. I strongly suggest you not take the hook. Restrain yourself, don't let zeal for reform influence you. Process challenges just don't work."

Consultant — "The campaigns that get help are the ones that listen to the [party committee] when they say that you have to go after a specific PAC and the like. The candidates that listen will get the help in the last few months of the campaign."

Until we change this kind of thinking in Washington, the situation will not improve. It is absolutely unthinkable that one of our major political parties would actually sponsor a seminar to educate would-be officeholders on how to get money from political action committees. The most amazing part of the story is that apparently there was no subtlety involved. The seminar might as well have been titled, "How To Sell Out in One Easy Lesson."

## An Assortment of Scandals

If the preceding story didn't make you somewhat skeptical about the way our government works, try these.

### THE SAVINGS AND LOAN SCANDAL

In 1984, our government was told of the savings and loan scandal. It was warned that if action were not taken promptly, the scandal would grow into a several-hundred-billion-dollar burden to the American taxpayer. Meanwhile, the PAC money kept flowing in from the Savings & Loans. Our elected servants and their staffs turned their backs on the impending disaster. Why? Because they were being flown around the country like royalty by the S&L crooks in their jets. Nobody did anything about the crisis until the day after the 1988 election — four years later.

Most of the savings and loan crooks never went to jail. The elected officials were never held accountable. Guess who bears the entire burden? American taxpayers are paying the tab to clean up this scandal, and will continue to pay. This is wrong.

### TAX AND BUDGET SUMMIT OF 1990

At the Tax and Budget Summit of 1990, the American people were promised that if we agreed to a tax increase, our federal budget would be balanced. Instead of balancing the budget, our elected servants increased spending $1.83 for every new dollar of tax increase, and the size of the debt continued to skyrocket. The people were conned by their elected servants.

This came on the heels of Congress giving itself a 23% pay raise earlier in the year, when hundreds of thousands of Americans were losing their jobs. The periodic pay raises that Congress approves for itself also contain cost-of-living adjustments similar to those given other federal employees. Cost-of-living increases on top of other salary increases are grossly unfair because the owners of the country, the American people, don't get cost-of-living increases when the dollar deteriorates. We feel the pain, while our federal servants get the gain. The people — the taxpayers — know this is unfair.

# GOOD PEOPLE, BAD SYSTEM

The people were also promised that both Congress and the White House would trim expenses, if we increased our taxes in 1991. Instead, the federal government continued to grow and spend. The elected officials, once again, ignored their promises.

Here are a few examples since 1991 —

- Senate employee benefits have increase 44%
- Congressional printing costs increased 48%
- Mail costs increased 44%
- The cost of employees in standing committees in the House alone increased 55%

Again, the people we elected to serve us did not keep their promises.

## CHECK-BOUNCING SCANDAL

As if Congress needed more negative publicity after the S&L scandal, news of the check-bouncing scandal was soon coming out of the nation's capital. This made the people even more skeptical and, I am sad to say, even cynical about their government. Our congressmen were writing personal checks on bank accounts they knew were overdrawn. The ordinary citizen could go to jail for this. In Washington, it was considered just another Congressional privilege. A cynic might be inclined to observe that Congress was only doing what it does every day — going into debt without worrying about when the money would get paid back.

## EXEMPTED FROM ITS OWN LAWS

This is difficult to believe, but Congress passes laws that apply to us but excludes itself. Some examples are:

- The Americans with Disabilities Act.
- The Equal Opportunity Act.

- The Occupational Safety and Health Act.
- Fair Labor Standards Act.

And, believe it or not, The Ethics in Government Act.

What are they thinking? Are they above the law? Are the laws so complicated that they want to be certain that they don't accidentally violate one? Are the laws such a nuisance and a bother that complying with them would be tedious and expensive? Welcome to the real world.

### POSTAGE STAMP SCANDAL

As this book goes to press, we are now faced with the stamp-cashing scandal, where a senior official in Congress is accused of obtaining $55,000 of stamps and turning them into cash. The Justice Department has been investigating this for months, and is about to reach a conclusion about whether or not to seek an injunction.

Now we have a Justice Department scandal, where the new Attorney General is firing the U.S. Attorney who has been involved in this situation.

We also have a unique situation where our new health care task force has refused to release the names of its members, and meets in secret. This group is not inventing a new nuclear weapon. Secrecy is not an issue in developing a new health care system. In fact, the whole process should be totally open so that the American people — the owners of this country — the people who are going to have to pay for it, understand the details of the new plan.

If police officers commit even the slightest indiscretion, they are punished — and even fired. We hold our people in the Armed Forces to very high ethical standards. Our most senior elected servants must maintain the highest ethical standards of all. They must lead by example. They don't.

## Government Waste

If you had a friend who overdrew his checking account on a regular basis, would you let him manage your money?

There is no discipline in our government when it comes to spending money.

The examples of government mismanagement and waste are everywhere. Here are just a few:

- The government owns 340,000 cars. This does not include military vehicles or postal vehicles. You and I have purchased one car for every ten government employees at a cost of $3 billion. It costs us $1 billion a year to keep them on the road.

- The 89th Airlift Wing takes care of the President's, Vice President's, and senior government officials' airplanes. It has 21 airplanes and 19 helicopters. Over 6,000 employees are involved in this activity, at an annual cost of $500 million. The Cold War is over. This operation must be dramatically reduced.

- In addition, the government owns and operates 1,200 civilian aircraft worth $2 billion, used to fly federal agency officials, their spouses and guests in royal comfort. This is ridiculous. Get rid of these aircraft, except for the President's. We can't afford these luxuries for our elected servants any longer. Have them go to the airport, get in line, lose their luggage, eat a bad meal, and get a taste of reality.

- Our government also leases 5,000 airplanes at an annual cost of $100 million. Cut it out.

- Our government gave away the cellular phone frequencies. These telephone frequencies are worth $32 billion today. Why did we give them away in a lottery instead of selling them to the end users, and using the money to pay down the debt?

- We spend $17 billion a year on job training. In some cases, 70% of the money goes to overhead and profit to the private contractors. This is not cost effective.

- Our government appropriated $5 billion for advertising American products around the world. Try to explain to a hardworking, taxpaying American why these profitable companies shouldn't buy their own ads.

- Our country has 4,000 public relations specialists on the payroll whose purpose is to present the government in the best possible light. We, the taxpayers, spend $800 million a year on people who tell us how great things are and why their agency needs more money. How dumb do they think we are? We don't need "Spin Doctors." We own this country. Just tell us the truth.

- The staffs of Congress and the White House staffs have mushroomed. For example:

  - In 1950, Congress had 6,700 staff members. This number has grown to over 30,000 in 1992.

  - Franklin Roosevelt fought and won World War II with a total staff of 200. Today, a very conservative number for the White House staff is 1,850, not counting over 1,000 full-time employees involved in White House Communications, and the U.S. Trade Representative, who has 147 staff members.

  - In addition, hundreds of people are carried on the books of other agencies, but are assigned to work at the White House for years.

  - In the recently announced White House staff cut, most of the fired staff were low-paid, career workers. Even though the number of persons cut was 25%, <u>the amount of money saved was only 5%</u>.

Government waste is symptomatic of a bad system, not bad people. The way the system works now, there is very little accountability by anyone. Until we make some fundamental changes to the system, we will continue to have gross government waste.

# NOT FOR SALE AT ANY PRICE

## It's Time for a Change

We must change the political process and create a government where people come to serve and then go back home. Service in government must not become a steppingstone to wealth and power. We must restructure our government so that the people in Washington work <u>for</u> us. They should be sensitive to <u>our</u> needs, and not be preoccupied with lobbyists from the special interest groups who provide them money for their next campaign. We must work to change the system.

THIS IS JOB ONE!

# Chapter Five

## A Giant Sucking Sound

As this book went to press, Congress was hearing testimony concerning the North American Free Trade Agreement, or NAFTA. If this agreement is signed as it is currently drafted, the next thing you hear will be a giant sucking sound as the remainder of our manufacturing jobs — what's left after the two million that went to Asia in the 1980s — get pulled across our southern border.

### From New Jersey to Mexico

Let's begin with a real-life story taken from *America: What Went Wrong?* by Donald L. Barlett and James B. Steele. Molly James lives in Paterson, New Jersey, in a modest house. She worked at Universal Manufacturing for thirty-three years making fluorescent lights. She was earning $7.91 an hour in 1986 when the company was sold to Drexel Burnham in a junk bond deal. Drexel and its partners put the new company heavily into debt. Everybody involved paid themselves huge fees.

# NOT FOR SALE AT ANY PRICE

On June 30, 1989, the plant in Paterson, New Jersey, was closed and moved to Mexico to achieve a dramatic increase in profitability because of the low wages paid Mexican workers. Molly, who was fifty-eight years old, lost her job and her health insurance when the plant closed .

In Mexico, Rosa Vasquez, age twenty-six, has Molly's old job. Rosa makes $59 a week. She and her family of four live in a one-room, 10 x 12 foot shack with no electricity or plumbing. They have an outdoor toilet and one kerosene lamp. This tiny, one-room shack is only reachable by walking along a dirt path. Chickens and pigs roam freely in the area. Everything Rosa makes goes just to try to feed and clothe her children.

What happened to the company? It earned record profits in 1991 after moving the Paterson plant to Mexico. It went public and the junk bond kings cashed in again. The chairman's former wife described their lifestyle in a divorce court proceeding. They lived in a $4 million mansion in Bel Air. They took vacations to Australia, Hong Kong, China, Japan, Paris, and London. They stayed in the best hotels and ate in the finest restaurants. They flew on the Concorde. Contrast their lives with those of Molly and Rosa.

Manufacturing gives us the tax base that enables us to pay our bills as a nation. Continuing to ship manufacturing facilities around the world or south of the border assures a dramatic annual growth in our national debt.

# A GIANT SUCKING SOUND

## For Our Own Protection

The new Administration is treating our uniformed forces in a scandalous manner. For example, a general was recently told by a young White House staffer when he appeared in uniform at the White House for a meeting. "Keep it short. We don't like uniforms in the White House." Put yourself in this officer's position. He has dedicated his life for his country. He has risked his life on the battlefield and now, as he nears retirement, he is subjected to this kind of abuse. The American people will not tolerate this. <u>This must stop</u>.

War is one of the constants of history. We would like to think there will be no more wars, but history teaches us there will be. The essential factor in winning World War II was our massive manufacturing capability. We cannot be a superpower or defend ourselves if we are not a major manufacturer.

Assume that we continue to ship entire industries to other countries and a major war breaks out ten years from now.

- We must go to Europe and respectfully ask, "May we have some steel?"
- We must go to the Middle East and beg the Arabs, "May we have some oil?"
- We must go to Asia and beg for integrated circuits.
- We must go to Asia and south of the border and beg, "Would you convert your car manufacturing plants to build military vehicles, tanks and aircraft for us?"

- We must go to Asia and south of the border and beg, "Would you make uniforms and boots for our troops?"
- We must go to Puerto Rico and beg for medicine and pharmaceuticals.

Surely, we are not so soft-headed that we will allow our great country to slip into this untenable situation.

## The View from Main Street

The North American Free Trade Agreement must be carefully evaluated. Let's begin by taking a look at the burdens that businesses in our country already carry.

- We pay manufacturing workers ten times what they make in Mexico.
- Our companies spend a great deal on health care, retirement, workers' compensation, life insurance, and many other benefits.
- The recently passed employee-leave bill adds to the cost of manufacturing.
- The minimum wage in the United States is $4.25. The Mexican minimum wage is 58¢.

The top job growth categories in the 1980s in our country were janitor/cleaner, food preparation worker, and cashier — honest work — but none of these jobs pay enough to support a family.

We have a history of one-sided trade agreements, where our nation and our people are placed at a distinct disadvantage. Entire industries have been lost overseas as a by-product of these agreements. Companies, cities and regions of the country have been damaged. We cannot pay our bills, balance the budget, and pay down our debt if our worker income base is deteriorating. We need a growing income base which gives us a growing tax base. Instead, at this critical time, our job and our tax base are deteriorating, because of past poorly conceived trade agreements and an adversarial relationship between government and business in our country.

Our successful competitors have an intelligent, supportive relationship between government and business. Their trade agreements are shrewdly calculated to benefit their people.

## The View from Wall Street

The capitalist's view and investor's view of NAFTA can best be summed up by a prospectus of an organization called Amerimex, created by Nafinsa, Mexico's largest state-owned development bank and the Warwick Group of New York.

- Amerimex planned to buy U.S. companies that are labor intensive and marginally profitable.
- The stock of these companies could be purchased at a very attractive price.
- The company's manufacturing operations would then be relocated to Mexico to take advantage of the reduced labor costs.

To quote from the prospectus:

> We estimate that manufacturing companies that experience fully loaded gross labor costs in the $7-$10 range in the U.S. may be able to utilize labor in Mexico at a fully loaded gross labor cost of $1.15 to $1.50 an hour. ...This could translate

into annual savings of $10,000 to $17,000 per employee, creating a dramatic increase in profitability.

The stock which had been purchased at a low price could then be sold at a dramatically higher price, as a result of moving the labor to Mexico. The characteristics of these companies are —

- Low to mid-range technology manufacturing.
- Moderate to good growth.
- Sales in the range of $10 million to $100 million.
- Excellent management and sales teams willing to remain with the company.
- Proven products.
- A labor component of 20% - 30% of the cost of goods sold.

United States companies meeting these criteria employ 5.8 million production workers in their plants and factories.

To me, this prospectus, which has now been withdrawn by Mexico because it so clearly summarized the impact of NAFTA on the United States, is the most succinct summary of the adverse impact of NAFTA on U.S. workers, and the U.S. tax base.

Both Mexico and the United States, as well as U.S. companies, have waged a huge lobbying effort in support of NAFTA. An article in the August 13, 1992, edition of the *New York Times* sums it up:

- People in key positions on the 1992 Presidential campaign have been retained as Mexican lobbyists.
- A former chief U.S. trade negotiator has been retained by the Mexican government and is being

paid several hundred thousand dollars a year for his services.

To quote the *New York Times:*

> The Salinas administration and its many lobbyists in Washington have fashioned what appears likely to be one of the most elaborate efforts at political persuasion ever undertaken in America by a foreign country.

> A Mexican official said, "We are going to be launching a strategy of being in almost the entire United States, meeting with the editorial boards of local newspapers, meeting with business chambers and talking with other people."

## The View from Mexico

Let's look at a few facts about Mexico:

- Northern Mexico is rapidly becoming the newest American industrial belt. Nearly 600,000 jobs have been located in Mexico that in the past might have been in the United States.
- Mexican workers can match the skills of 70% of the labor force in the United States.
- To maintain the low wages that draw American companies to Mexico, President Salinas has gotten commitments from business and union leaders to limit raises.
- "It could be years before the gap with American wages narrows significantly," said the chairman of Zenith Electric Corporation, which has 20,000 employees in Mexico.

# NOT FOR SALE AT ANY PRICE

- Auto makers have 64 plants in Mexico.

Take a look at some examples of working and living conditions in Mexico:

- Workers at a U.S. assembly plant in Juarez are paid 58¢ an hour — Mexico's minimum wage.
- Mexican workers' salaries fell 65% in real terms during the 1980's.
- In one strike concluded in 1990, dozens of workers were shot and injured by state police. The plant was shut down. Two thousand workers were fired, and those who remained had a 45% pay cut from $2.64 to $1.45 per hour.
- More than 14,000 plant workers were fired at a European-owned plant and the union dissolved. Former union leaders signed a new contract without consulting the workers.
- Safety standards are minimal.
- Mexican workers who are injured on the job are limited to $10,127 in worker compensation claims.
- Death benefits are capped at $6,720. A life insurance policy paid $650 and a $23-a-month pension.
- Blue-collar jobs in Mexico now pay only 3.4% more than they did four years ago, while inflation was almost 12% in just the past year.
- Many Mexican workers with U.S. companies cannot qualify for government housing credits and instead scavenge cardboard and trash to build homes. To buy a low-income house, a minimum wage earner would have to work 200 years.

# A GIANT SUCKING SOUND

Compare conditions in automobile assembly plants in Mexico with those in the United States:

- Production workers are high school or technical school graduates, hired for the assembly line at $1.55 an hour. U.S. auto workers are paid $16.00 an hour.
- This Mexican wage rate does not cover food and housing costs for a family of five, estimated at $15 a day.
- A Mexican engineering graduate can expect to earn $5,000 per year at one of the factories upon graduation. Engineering graduates in the United States can expect starting salaries of $25,000 to $30,000 per year.

## To Accept or Reject

We have heard a great deal of talk about NAFTA creating new jobs in the United States — such as selling machine tools and helping Mexico build new factories. Think it through. These are one-time jobs. Wouldn't it be better to have the factories here, employing people for several decades rather than having one-time jobs helping Mexico get into the manufacturing business?

The North American Free Trade Agreement was created before President Clinton took office. The challenge for our new President and his chief trade negotiator is to carefully consider the Agreement that was presented to them when they took office.

As I understand it, Congress is not allowed to make changes to the Agreement, and can only vote to accept or reject the agreement. I am confident that both the

# NOT FOR SALE AT ANY PRICE

President and Mr. Kantor will work to assure that the agreement is fair and that the interests of the American people are protected. Unfortunately, this has not been our pattern as a country in the past, and has resulted in significant damage to both our country and its people.

The core question is, "How do we resolve the problems that are fundamentally driven by a huge gap in pay?" Obviously, we cannot implode our job base and tax base at this critical moment.

Don't you find it interesting and irrational that, at the same time our leaders are talking about creating inner city jobs and enterprise zones, we stifle small business development and ship millions of jobs overseas?

Mexico has some of the least costly workers in the world. Our country has the world's most productive work force, but it is expensive. U.S. workers will lose because of the sizable wage difference. Our country will also incur a tremendous loss in taxes and increase in welfare payments due to lost jobs at a time when we need a growing tax base to pay our bills.

One-half of Mexico's population is fifteen years old or younger. One million new workers enter the Mexican labor force each year. Mexico can absorb huge numbers of new jobs every year at 58¢ per hour with just these new workers.

Economic models have been developed showing that this is a favorable plan for the United States. These economic models make a number of unrealistic assumptions, such as a full-employment assumption: any American losing a job immediately gets a new job. That is not the way it works. Just look back at the 1980s.

We can either delay NAFTA and correct its deficiencies or ratify it and try to work out these problems with supplemental agreements. We lose all leverage once we have ratified the agreement. Mexico will have no incentive to give up its advantage. In all probability, the problems in the current agreement will never by satisfactorily resolved, and will create stress between our countries.

We need jobs here, and we must manufacture here if we wish to remain a superpower. We must stop shipping manufacturing jobs overseas and once again make the words "Made in the USA" the world's standard of excellence.

We can do it.

The question is — will we?

It's up to us, the owners of this country —
THE PEOPLE.

# Chapter Six

## The Challenge

The American people have a rare opportunity to actually reform our political system. During the next few months, Congress will be deciding upon taxing and spending measures. There will never be a better time to tell Congress what we want from our government in exchange for the higher taxes that we are getting ready to pay. Here are ten specific proposals for reform that will go a long way toward solving many of the problems that plague the current political system, and that will help to correct our economic problems at the same time.

In a poll conducted March 21-22, 1993, by the Gordon S. Black Corporation, citizens across the country were asked to respond to questions about government reform. Their responses are shown in the proposals listed below.

BEFORE WE, THE PEOPLE, WILL AGREE TO A TAX INCREASE — WE DEMAND THE FOLLOWING REFORMS:

## Reform Proposal #1

Give the American people the detailed financial plan for tax increases, spending increases, and spending cuts.

- We have no interest in raising taxes now, with only a vague promise that spending cuts will be made later.
- Give us a detailed time schedule with 90-day benchmarks so that we can compare the projections for the program with actual results.
- Detail how the plan will lead to elimination of deficit spending in the near-term and debt reduction in the long-term.
- As you spend our money, be careful — not reckless, as you have been in the past.

89% FAVOR PRESENTING THE ENTIRE FINANCIAL PLAN TO THE AMERICAN PEOPLE SO THAT THE NET RESULTS OF THE PLAN ARE SEEN BEFORE PEOPLE ARE ASKED TO PAY HIGHER TAXES.

## Reform Proposal #2

Publish an accurate, audited quarterly financial report that will allow the taxpayers to see the actual results and determine whether or not the plan is producing the promised results in connection with taxing, spending, and savings.

- This quarterly financial statement will be our instrument panel to see whether or not our leaders are performing on budget, and on schedule.

# THE CHALLENGE

- All results must be accurately accounted for. Stop rounding off to the nearest tens or hundreds of billions of dollars. Don't give us estimates, give us accurate numbers.
- Eliminate all off-balance-sheet items and other accounting tricks. For example, do not call an increase in Social Security taxes a "savings." Call it what it is — a tax increase.
- Never again try to manipulate us with funny numbers or confusing phrases such as "revenue enhancement." Just call it what it is — a tax increase.

92% FAVOR A PROPOSAL FOR A QUARTERLY, AUDITED FINANCIAL REPORT SO THAT WE CAN KNOW WHETHER THE RESULTS OF DEFICIT REDUCTION PROGRAMS ARE BEING ACHIEVED.

## Reform Proposal #3

Pass the Balanced Budget Amendment to the Constitution.

- There is no financial discipline in Washington. The only way to get our elected servants to balance the budget and get rid of the debt is to pass the Balanced Budget Amendment to the Constitution.
- A deficit-phase-down period of no more than five years should be included to avoid damaging the economy.
- An emergency clause should be included that allows a deficit only in the event of a major military conflict.
- Any non-military emergencies will require immediate spending cuts or a tax increase.

# NOT FOR SALE AT ANY PRICE

## 71% FAVOR A BALANCED BUDGET AMENDMENT.

## Reform Proposal #4

Give the President the Line Item Veto.

- To make balancing the budget a reality, we need to give the President the Line Item Veto.
- Many states already have a balanced budget provision, and several have given their governors the power to enforce it with the Line Item Veto.
- The Line Item Veto will allow the President to kill pork-barrel projects which members of Congress try to push through the system by attaching them to other pieces of legislation.

### 61% FAVOR THE LINE ITEM VETO.

## Reform Proposal #5

Pass a term limitation law as part of the tax increase package.

- If the financial forecast which Congress approves does not produce results on schedule, a term limitation law would automatically take effect and limit the number of terms members of Congress can serve.
- This creates an incentive for our elected representatives to keep their promises.

# THE CHALLENGE

78% FAVOR A TERM LIMITATION LAW THAT AUTOMATICALLY TAKES EFFECT IF CONGRESS FAILS TO MEET A PUBLICLY AGREED UPON DEFICIT REDUCTION TIMETABLE.

## Reform Proposal #6

Eliminate foreign lobbyists. Curtail domestic lobbyists.
- Create criminal penalties for anyone involved in foreign lobbying activities.
- At the same time, curtail the activities of domestic lobbyists to providing information; eliminate all possibility of lobbyists giving money to or raising money for campaigns — directly or indirectly.

67% FAVOR THE ELIMINATION OF FOREIGN LOBBYISTS

78% FAVOR REDUCING THE ROLE OF DOMESTIC LOBBYISTS.

75% BELIEVE THAT FOREIGN LOBBYISTS HAVE TOO MUCH INFLUENCE OVER PUBLIC POLICY.

## Reform Proposal #7

Change federal election laws to eliminate the influence of the special interests.
- Get rid of all political action committees.
- Replace the electoral college with the popular vote.
- Get rid of all "soft money" contributions to political parties.

- Shorten the time for political campaigns. This will reduce the cost, and therefore the need to raise huge sums of money.

### 69% FAVOR THE ELIMINATION OF POLITICAL ACTION COMMITTEES.

### 74% BELIEVE THAT CAMPAIGN CONTRIBUTIONS FROM POLITICAL ACTION COMMITTEES HAVE TOO MUCH INFLUENCE OVER OUR PUBLIC POLICY.

## Reform Proposal #8

The American people are being asked to sacrifice. Our elected leaders in Washington must lead by example — all sacrifice must start at the top.

- Cut the President's and Congressional salaries by at least 10%.
- Cut staff costs by 25%.
- Eliminate all automatic cost-of-living adjustments for federal employees — taxpayers don't get them. Congress has no incentive to keep the dollar strong.
- Today, ninety members of Congress have retirement plans worth over two million dollars each. Bring the congressional retirement plan in line with the retirement plans of the American people they were elected to serve.
- Eliminate perks such as subsidized haircuts, subsidized food, and free parking at National Airport.
- Eliminate limousines and chauffeurs — except for the President and a small number of other senior officials with major security problems.

# THE CHALLENGE

- Sell the 1,200 government airplanes now used to fly senior officials around.
- Close vacation retreats paid for by the people, but available only to senior public officials.
- Do not pass legislation which applies to us and not to Congress.
- Pass a law which requires Congress to abide by the same laws as the people, including those laws from which Congress has previously exempted itself.
- Dramatically slash the cost of the President's aircraft — 21 airplanes - 19 helicopters - 6,000 staff members - $500 million per year budget.

90% FAVOR THE SALARY REDUCTION PROPOSAL.

89% FAVOR THE ELIMINATION OF PERKS AND SPECIAL PRIVILEGES.

90% FAVOR THE PROPOSAL OF REDUCING THE RETIREMENT PLANS OF CONGRESS TO BRING THEM IN LINE WITH AMERICAN WORKERS.

## Reform Proposal #9

Institute pilot programs for major new spending initiatives, such as health care.
- First of all, explain major, new spending programs in detail before passing them into law.
- Before implementing these complex and expensive programs, conduct pilot programs. Make sure these new programs work.
- Report the costs and benefits of the pilot programs in detail to the people.

- If the pilot programs work as planned, they can then be implemented with little risk of failure.
- Finally, make these new programs dynamic, allowing the administrators to improve and optimize them based on actual experience.

**93% BELIEVE THAT MAJOR NEW PROGRAMS SHOULD FIRST BE PRESENTED TO THE AMERICAN PEOPLE IN DETAIL BEFORE THEY ARE IMPLEMENTED NATIONWIDE.**

**85% BELIEVE THAT PROGRAMS SHOULD BE TESTED IN PILOT PROGRAMS TO PROVE THEIR EFFECTIVENESS BEFORE THEY ARE IMPLEMENTED NATIONWIDE.**

---

## Reform Proposal #10

Don't get caught up in the "First 100 Days" mindset.
- Don't try to do too many things at once.
- Poorly conceived legislation will be rushed through with the costs understated and the benefits overstated.
- The American people will pay more money than anticipated for programs that are second-rate.
- To use an old carpenter's saying, "Measure twice — cut once."

I realize that this may seem to be strong medicine to our senior elected servants. As they consider this plan, we remind them to never forget that they have badly mismanaged our money. From now on we demand that they treat it as a limited resource — stop wasting our money.

Finally, we direct them to earn our trust and respect by conducting their business in an honest and ethical manner. They can begin to do this by making certain that the taxpayers are provided with accurate and timely information about the country's financial situation.

# Chapter Seven

## United We Stand America

The purpose of United We Stand America is to give the people a voice.

You own United We Stand America.

The goals of United We Stand America are:

- To re-create a government that comes from the people — not at the people.

- To reform the federal government at all levels to eliminate fraud, waste, and abuse.

- To have a government where the elected, appointed, and career officials come to serve and not to cash in.

- To get our economy moving and put our people back to work.

- To balance the budget.

- To pay off our nation's debt.

- To build an efficient and cost effective health care system.

- To get rid of foreign lobbyists.

- To get rid of political action committees.

- To make our neighborhoods and streets safe from crime and violence.

- To create the finest public schools in the world for our children.

- To pass on the American Dream to our children, making whatever fair shared sacrifices are necessary.

The annual membership fee is $15.00. An application is included at the back of this book.

The relevant question is: Are you willing to spend the cost of two movie tickets and a bag of popcorn to rebuild your country and pass on the American Dream to your children? The money will be carefully spent to build a nationwide, grassroots organization and sponsor electronic town halls.

What kind of organization will United We Stand America become? The members of United We Stand America will join together to —

- Serve their country in a selfless manner;

- Seek no personal gain, except to have a better country to pass on to our children;

- Work night and day to avoid the turf battles and endless fighting that seems inherent in other political organizations;

- Select leaders who, by example, exhibit the qualities needed to make the organization successful;

- Build chapters in every city, town, and neighborhood in the country;

- Have people look upon this organization as they do the Salvation Army — good, hardworking, decent, caring people who have come together for a good cause, the future of our country.

The initial membership campaign will continue for several months. It is a massive undertaking by the volunteers who have proven their capabilities. There is no question in my mind that you will succeed in accomplishing these objectives.

## The First National Referendum

On March 21, 1993, United We Stand America presented a 30-minute television program titled "The First National Referendum." I hosted the program, and spoke about the need for government reform. In the poll conducted immediately after the program and the next day by the Gordon S. Black Corporation, the American public was asked for its reaction to the television show. Here is their response.

- 89% favored our message;
- 86% thought United We Stand America should sponsor more shows in the future;

- 79% favor the creation of a nationwide citizens organization to involve people in political and budgetary reform.

In a separate poll conducted by CNN and *USA Today* shortly after the television program, only 23% of the American public have confidence that our government does the right thing all or most of the time. The same poll gave United We Stand America a favorable rating of 66%.

Mr. Black also noted that 20% of all respondents, not just those who had seen the television program, said they planned to join United We Stand America. He concludes:

It appears that more than 20 million adults heard or watched Mr. Perot's broadcast. . . . If anywhere near the 20% join United We Stand America, it will have succeeded in creating the largest citizens' organization in the history of the United States. An organization with 20 million or more adults will be larger than the entire labor movement in the United States, and it will have the potential to be the most influential organization ever.

United We Stand America is well on its way to becoming a powerful voice in the political and economic future of our country.

Finally, I would again like to thank the volunteers for their brilliant efforts, their patriotism, their love for this country, and their devotion to their families. You have created United We Stand America for the American people and future generations of Americans.

# United We Stand America
# Founding Member Application
### Make copies of this page to give to your friends

I WANT MY VOICE TO BE HEARD. PLEASE ENROLL ME AS A FOUNDING MEMBER OF UNITED WE STAND AMERICA. I WILL BE PART OF THIS NATIONAL COALITION WORKING TO BRING ABOUT THE NECESSARY REFORMS IN OUR NATION'S ECONOMY, GOVERNMENT, AND ELECTION LAWS.

❑ Enclosed is my check for $15 payable to United We Stand America, Inc.

❑ **Mr.**
❑ **Mrs.**
❑ **Ms.** _____

       First         Middle Initial        Last

_____

Street Address                    Apt. #

_____

City            State         Zip Code

_____

Home Phone   (include area codes)     Work Phone

❑ I would also like to become a volunteer in my state.

❑ In addition to becoming a founding member of United We Stand America, I would like to make the following contribution to United We Stand America, Inc. to further its goals and objectives:

❑ **$25**    ❑ **$50**    ❑ **$100**    **Other $_____**

**Gift Memberships.** You can give a membership as a gift. Include your name, address and the above information for each person on a separate piece of paper and enclose $15 for each membership. A membership card will be sent to each gift recipient.

### How to Join

1. Fill out enrollment form completely. Please print.
2. Cut out form, and mail with your check or money order made payable to United We Stand America, Inc.
3. Affix postage and mail to the address provided below. Postal Service will not deliver without proper postage.

**Contribution and membership fees are not tax deductible, nor will they be used to defray any expense of the Perot '92 Campaign**

# United We Stand America, Inc.
## Dept. 3000, P.O. Box 6, Dallas, Texas 75221